Jack Skeen | Greg Miller | Aaron Hill

THE

POWER

WORKBOOK

Part of the Circle Blueprint System

Published by:
Griffin Publishing
314 E. Lake Shore Drive
Tower Lakes, IL 60010
Phone: (847) 910-1640

ISBN: 978-0-9993388-2-7

Library of Congress Control Number: 2017956815

Printed in the United States of America

TABLE OF CONTENTS

INTRODUCTION
TO POWER

INTRODUCTION TO POWER

The Power Workbook offers a system to help you decode the conscious and unconscious factors that affect your success. Power is the second of four fundamental development areas of *The Circle Blueprint* —which you may have read, but which is not entirely essential. There are also workbooks for the other three fundamental development areas (Independence, Humility, and Purpose), and you may wish to also work through the Independence Workbook before this workbook as well as move onto the others after you complete the Power Workbook to more fully develop your Circle Blueprint. The system in this workbook is intended for anyone with an interest in developing a higher mastery of the element of Power. We each possess gifts like special qualities and skills that offer value to us and the world—we like to call these Power and people who develop a mastery of Power put their gifts and qualities on display for the world!

ASSESSING YOUR POWER

If you have read *The Circle Blueprint*, you are likely familiar with the self-assessment tool available at www.thecircleblueprint.com. This tool, which we will explain below for those who are who are either unfamiliar or who want a reminder, helps you understand where you are on various factors that constitute the element of Power. If you are comfortable with the assessment process, you may want to proceed to the After Self-Assessment section.

POWER CONSISTS OF SIX FACTORS:

1. **Self-Determination:** Establishing your own goals and moving steadily toward them.

2. **Self-Efficacy:** Belief in yourself.

3. **Achievement-Striving:** Ability to direct your energy and skills in a way that can bring about positive outcomes.

4. **Zest:** Exuding enthusiasm and breathing energy into life.

5. **Acceptance:** An openness to change and differences.

6. **Self-Discipline:** Ability to do the things that need to be done.

The Circle Blueprint provides in-depth explanations of these factors, but this overview should give you the gist of it, and the results of your assessment, or even honest self-reflection on these issues, will let you know where you may need further development or better balance.

Specifically, the assessment results provide descriptions on our "Thriving Scale." On each factor, you should have a score.

1. I am *hanging on* by my fingernails. Despite all I have accomplished, my life isn't good at all.

2. I am *eroding*. I'm not desperate, but my life is a grind and does not seem to be headed in a positive direction.

3. I am *treading water* and just sort of enduring my situation. My life isn't bad, but I would not say it is good, either.

4. I am *growing*. My life is on a positive trajectory. Certainly, it could be better, but I am reasonably satisfied and optimistic about the future.

5. I am *thriving*. I am creatively engaged in my work and life. I am at the top of my game. I feel energized, balanced, healthy, and happy.

AFTER SELF-ASSESSMENT

Once you have an idea of where you are on each factor, you can proceed to the exercise series. We have broken these out according to where you fall on the Thriving Scale. In this way, you can go through various exercises according to where you are. That is, if you are hanging on, complete the exercises that align with hanging on, and if you are growing, you can complete the exercises that align with growing. There are no exercises for areas where you are thriving because you do not need further development in those factors. We have included multiple sessions to allow you to work on developing each factor over time. After you complete Session 1, you can move to Session 2 and so on. Further, you can also repeat the assessment or even work on your own development over time—after you complete the "treading water" exercises, for example, you can move onto the "growing" exercises. We have often found it helpful to revisit the exercises at one level of the Thriving Scale a few times if need be, and in other instances, just moving to the next level after one pass may be sufficient. The system is flexible for you and 100 percent self-driven—you complete the exercise series as you see fit, but this offers you a system for developing your Circle Blueprint at your own pace and in total privacy.

EXERCISE SERIES: SELF-DETERMINATION

FACTOR – SELF-DETERMINATION

This factor focuses on the ability to think and act on behalf of yourself. It is not selfishness, but the ability to balance your desires and goals with those of the broader community in such a way that you are able to continue to grow, develop, and be fully self-expressed. Self-determined people are those who have the ability to lead others because they are not enmeshed in the neediness of dependency.

SELF-ASSESSED RATING – HANGING ON

Instead of running your life, your life is completely running you. You feel fully at the effect of your circumstances.

SESSION 1

EXERCISE 1A – SELF-DETERMINATION, HANGING ON

Thinking you have no control. You are hanging on by your fingernails because you have almost completely surrendered your self-determination. Instead of running your life, your life is running you. In Session 1 we invite you to focus on the experience of being out of control of your own life. Let's get started.

Exercise 1 asks you to focus on your thoughts. When you lack self-determination, it seems as if there is nothing you can do to manage your life. It is like you are on a bus being driven by someone else. You are on a journey, but not one of your own making. It is important to become aware of the thoughts that pass through your mind throughout the day to bring to your attention how much you see your life as out of your own control.

TASK: Begin a diary and make a list of the thoughts you have about your life not being under your control.

EXERCISE 2A – SELF-DETERMINATION, HANGING ON

Exercise 2 invites you to become aware of the feeling of helplessness. Helplessness tends to breed apathy and undermines even the most basic choices for self-care. And, helplessness can be insidious as it quietly dominates your mood. Again, use your diary to become aware of your feelings. Helplessness will show up as sadness, hopelessness, and apathy.

TASK: Write down every time you experience one of these emotional states and what is occurring when you have it. Can you begin to see a pattern of feeling helpless that has been undermining your life? It is this feeling that you will need to address.

EXERCISE 3A – SELF-DETERMINATION, HANGING ON

Exercise 3 invites you to focus on your behavior. When you are hanging on by your fingernails, it is easy to fall into a pattern of waiting to see what will occur rather than shaping your future. Your behavior will tend to be passive and accepting as though nothing can be done to make things better. Passive acceptance shows up in laziness, procrastination, and self-indulgent habits like overeating, excessive consumption of alcohol, and using drugs. None of these behaviors are of any benefit to you. They fill your time without making any improvement.

TASK: Use your diary to track your time. How much of your time is spent being passive instead of being constructive?

EXERCISE 4A – SELF-DETERMINATION, HANGING ON

Exercise 4 invites you to notice your habits or your adaptation to your situation. When you are hanging on by your fingernails, it is easy to fall into the habit of reacting to what is occurring rather than creating what you want. Problems feel overwhelming, as if you have no ability to deal with them. Circumstances seem impossible to change. Life becomes a habit pattern that spirals into less and less active, functional, and adaptive behavior.

TASK: Look back over the past five years. Write down any habit patterns that are leading you toward less functionality. Each one of these will need to be addressed for you to turn your life around.

SESSION 2
EXERCISE 1B – SELF-DETERMINATION, HANGING ON

Session 2 focuses on changes that need to occur in your thinking, feeling, behavior, and habit patterns in order to stop your decline and prepare you for changing your life for the better.

Exercise 1 invites you to shift your thinking pattern from thinking you have no control to thinking that you are very much in control. This is a very big shift and will require the cultivation of some new patterns of viewing yourself and the world around you. Let's get started. Pick one area in which you think you have no control. It might be your vocation. It might seem like you are trapped in your job. Or, you might be in a relationship that is holding you back. Write down whatever circumstance comes to mind. Notice that you don't see any options for change. Now, go sit in a different chair. We will call this chair the chair of possibilities. Look at the situation where you think you are trapped.

TASK: Write down as many options for resolving the situation that you can think of. Don't be practical. Don't limit yourself. Don't be realistic. The goal of this exercise is for you to see that there are almost always options. Sometimes the price you must pay for some of these options is high, but there are usually things you can do that you have not done yet to make your life better.

EXERCISE 2B – SELF-DETERMINATION, HANGING ON

Exercise 2 invites you to take control of your emotional state. Feelings can sometimes be so powerful that they create your reality. If you feel hopeless, you will be hopeless. But, feelings are actually the result of our interpretation of our situation. They come from all that we say inside our head about ourselves and our circumstances. It is important that we manage our feelings rather than allowing our feelings to manage our lives. In the last exercise, you made a list of some thoughts that could actually improve your situation even though they "feel" impossible, impractical, or too costly. Perhaps that feeling isn't correct.

TASK: Practice telling yourself a different story about these options. Review each one and tell yourself why it might actually be a good idea. Notice that your feelings tend to shift from being hopeless to being ever so slightly hopeful.

EXERCISE 3B – SELF-DETERMINATION, HANGING ON

Exercise 3 focuses on your behavior. When you feel hopeless, you will tend to be passive, as if waiting to see what will happen. Waiting can actually increase anxiety because it allows you to imagine all kinds of negative possibilities. A major shift in behavior is going from waiting to taking action, even if it is a very small step. Moving forward creates momentum that can build on itself. When you are accustomed to being passive, the best way to begin moving forward is to focus on the smallest first step.

TASK: What is the easiest thing you can do to put one of your options for change into play? Write it down. Now, commit to doing it. Don't let your feelings talk you out of it.

EXERCISE 4B – SELF-DETERMINATION, HANGING ON

Exercise 4 invites you to begin changing habits are undermining your well-being. Habits are like ruts you grow accustomed to, and for that reason, they are often difficult to break out of. Instead of breaking a bad habit, it is more useful to substitute a better habit for the old one. For example, if you want to give up smoking, rather than simply trying to stop, it would be better to plan a new activity at the times when you usually smoked. Building a new (non-smoking) habit crowds out the old one.

TASK: Take one of your bad habits from the list you constructed during Session 1. First, decide if you are ready to change it. If you aren't, pick a different one. If you are, consider a new habit that would be a good replacement for the old one. Write it down and begin building it.

SESSION 3
EXERCISE 1C – SELF-DETERMINATION, HANGING ON

Stop giving up control of your life to all external forces and pressures. This is a necessary first step toward self-determination.

Exercise 1 asks you to focus on ways you might be allowing yourself to be controlled by your past. When your life has been declining, it is easy to begin to feel like the deck is stacked against you and your past difficulties are predictive of your future. However, allowing the past to dictate your future is a huge mistake. What occurred in the past has nothing to do with what you can create for yourself today and tomorrow. It is critical that you leave the past behind you, and free yourself from any sense that it controls your life now.

TASK: Take out a sheet of paper and write at the top, "My Life Starts Today." This sheet of paper symbolizes your life free from the past and open to whatever possibilities you wish to create. Now, write down whatever comes to mind that you want to create in your life going forward.

EXERCISE 2C – SELF-DETERMINATION, HANGING ON

Exercise 2 asks you to focus on any control of your life you have given over to others. You may have been living in fear of what your boss, spouse, or friend might do if you gave up pleasing them or made some other change that would make your life more functional. You may have been worried about the consequences to someone in your life if you didn't continue to meet their needs, even when doing so is not the best thing for you. In truth, the only life you can save is your own. No relationship is as important as your relationship with yourself.

TASK: Make a list of all of the people in your life who weaken you or undermine your success. You will need to begin separating yourself from each of these people and replacing these relationships with ones that are more helpful and functional.

EXERCISE 3C – SELF-DETERMINATION, HANGING ON

Exercise 3 invites you to focus on any circumstance or circumstances that undermine your well-being. You may be in the wrong job, such that every day is a grind. You might be living in the wrong neighborhood and the influences around you tempt you into poor behavior. You might be in a bad relationship; one in which you are sacrificing your aliveness because you are too afraid of what might happen if you speak up.

TASK: Make a list of all circumstances you have allowed to undermine your life. You must now make a plan to change them. Change can be hard, but these changes are necessary. When you have made these changes, you will feel your life getting stronger.

EXERCISE 4C – SELF-DETERMINATION, HANGING ON

Exercise 4 invites you to take control of any and all habits that are causing your life to be in disrepair. Trying to improve your life while you are maintaining bad habits is like trying to fill a tire with air while it has a leak. No matter how hard you work, you can't sustain your progress. Eventually, you will give up and fall back into your weak position. So, we ask you to make a list of all of your bad habits; those that rob you of your vitality and life. If you are going to take charge of your life, you must first put these bad habits behind you. Often this requires a great deal of support from others as well as making some new choices as to how you spend your time.

TASK: For each of your bad habits, create a new, healthier habit that you will cultivate in its place. List the people you will depend on for support as you make these changes.

SESSION 4

EXERCISE 1D – SELF-DETERMINATION, HANGING ON

Session 4 will focus on concrete ways to begin exerting self-determination in your life.

Exercise 1 invites you to make a clear decision to take responsibility for your life. Surrendering control of your life to circumstances outside yourself can be subtle and insidious. You may not have even realized how much responsibility for your own welfare you have given up. Now, it is time for you to take back all that you have given away. You can do this by writing a mission statement for yourself. It may read something like this, "From this day forward, I take 100 percent responsibility for my own well-being. I will not blame anyone or anything for the state of my life. I will now make decisions that advance my life and well-being."

TASK: Write it down. Review it each day. Post it somewhere you will see it daily.

EXERCISE 2D – SELF-DETERMINATION, HANGING ON

Exercise 2 invites you to take on low-hanging fruit; issues you can solve quickly that immediately begin to demonstrate you are taking control of your life. Almost everyone has things they do that get in the way of forward progress and/or things they could do that will make their lives better. These could be as simple as eating junk food, sleeping past your alarm, cheating on your hours at work, or not exercising.

TASK: Make a list of the things you could easily either give up or start doing that you know will be good for you. Now, do them. You will immediately begin to experience the benefits of having increased your self-determination. Your confidence will improve. You will encourage yourself to continue to expand your control over your life.

EXERCISE 3D – SELF-DETERMINATION, HANGING ON

Exercise 3 invites you to take on one more difficult goal. This might be some persistent habit that has been holding you back. For example, you might be overweight and know you need to lose it, but have been ignoring the issue. Or, you might know you need to find a more satisfying job, but you have been lazy and haven't done anything.

TASK: Make a list of all of the issues of this sort you need to address in order for your life to be thriving. Now, pick one. We want you to focus on solving this problem. Don't let yourself get distracted. Don't try to solve other things. Put all of your energy on addressing this issue. Set a clear and measurable goal. Establish a date for when you will reach your goal. Create a plan that includes all of the steps necessary to achieve the goal. Get to work!

EXERCISE 4D – SELF-DETERMINATION, HANGING ON

Exercise 4 invites you to review your progress and to celebrate your success. Regaining control of your life must be fed by celebrating your successes. When you see that the decisions you made actually improved your life, you will be encouraged to keep moving forward. Retaking control of your life is a step-by-step process that requires slow and steady progress.

TASK: Make a list of the changes you have made as a result of these exercises. What new decisions have you made? What new changes have you made? What has resulted from them? Take time to be proud of yourself for all that you have done to improve your life. Enjoy that feeling throughout the week.

FACTOR – SELF-DETERMINATION

This factor focuses on the ability to think and act on behalf of yourself. It is not selfishness, but the ability to balance your desires and goals with those of the broader community in such a way that you are able to continue to grow, develop, and be fully self-expressed. Self-determined people are those who have the ability to lead others because they are not enmeshed in the neediness of dependency.

SELF-ASSESSED RATING – ERODING

You have control of some aspects of your life, but are progressively feeling at the effect of external forces you don't control.

SESSION 1
EXERCISE 1A – SELF-DETERMINATION, ERODING

Your life is eroding because you have been substantially surrendering your self-determination. Instead of running your life, you have been allowing circumstances and other people to run it. In Session 1 we invite you to focus on the experience of giving over control of your life to outside forces. Let's get started.

Exercise 1 asks you to focus on your thoughts. When you are surrendering your self-determination, it seems as if winning the game of life is simply too hard. Perhaps in the past you believed you could continually improve your situation and the quality of your life, but you have gone through a series of failures and disappointments and, in the process, lost track of your positive belief. It is critically important that you become aware of the thoughts that lead you to surrender your self-determination. Begin a diary to track your thoughts.

TASK: Write down every thought you have that expresses the idea that it isn't worth trying to manage your life. These thoughts undermine positive change and must be managed.

EXERCISE 2A – SELF-DETERMINATION, ERODING

Exercise 2 invites you to become aware of your feelings. Your feelings either support positive change or surrender your self-determination. Feelings of being scared or angry suggest you are living at the effect of life rather than with the confidence that you can manage your life toward a positive outcome.

TASK: This week use your diary to track your emotions. Write down every time you are feeling angry or scared. Write the object of your anger or fear. It will be difficult to regain your self-determination until you free yourself from these negative emotions and substitute emotions like hope and joy.

EXERCISE 3A – SELF-DETERMINATION, ERODING

Exercise 3 invites you to become aware of your behavior. How are you acting toward yourself and your life? Your behavior becomes a series of choices that lead to patterns that can be difficult to change. Since you are eroding, it is likely that instead of actively shaping your life every day, you are frequently submissive, as though it is better for you to fit into whatever comes your way. Having gone through difficulties, it is almost as if you are expecting them to show up at any time, and so you see no value in working to make your situation better. Passivity might show up in self-indulgent behavior such as wasting time on meaningless activities that accomplish little or nothing.

TASK: Use your diary this week to track how you invest your time. Notice how much time you are spending on activities that are not helpful in improving your situation. Wasted time is a valuable resource you will need to capture and put to use as you move your life in the direction of thriving.

EXERCISE 4A – SELF-DETERMINATION, ERODING

As mentioned in Exercise 3, choices can become habits that are difficult to change. Exercise 4 invites you to focus on any habits you may have developed that are undermining your self-determination. One of the easiest habits to fall into when your life is eroding is to act as if you don't have control over your life. When playing the victim becomes a habit, life appears to be more difficult that it actually is. You train yourself to see the obstacles and not the opportunities. Your point of view justifies doing little to manage your life.

TASK: Use your diary to make a list of any bad habits that are currently undermining your functionality. How much of your time is spent on bad habits?

SESSION 2
EXERCISE 1B – SELF-DETERMINATION, ERODING

Session 2 is designed to help you begin to change your thinking, feelings, behaviors, and habits in the direction of increased self-determination. Let's get started.

Exercise 1 invites you to focus on altering your thinking. As you discovered in Exercise 1 of Session 1, a great deal of your thinking is dominated by the idea that there is no way for you to win the game of life. You believe others can improve their lives but not you. You see yourself as having bad luck or dealt a bad hand. Such thinking will actually attract the misfortune you need to avoid. It is time for you to begin taking control of your thoughts and to focus them on the idea that everyone can have an amazing life, and that includes you.

TASK: Get out a sheet of paper and write down ten statements that affirm you and your ability to shape your life. You don't have to believe them at this point. Just get creative and write them down. If you can't come up with ten, continue this exercise every day until you have ten. They can be statements like, "I am a capable person." Or, "I am smart enough to have whatever I want." When you have ten, read this list out loud three times each day for the next thirty days. As you read the statements, imagine that they are completely true. By doing so, you are training your mind to think in ways that support your success.

EXERCISE 2B – SELF-DETERMINATION, ERODING

Exercise 2 invites you to shape your emotions to support your self-determination. In Exercise 1 of Session 1, you identified some emotions that weaken your self-determination. Being frightened and/or angry keeps you trapped in feeling like a victim to others and/or to your circumstances. You became aware of how often you experience those negative and counterproductive emotions. Now, we want you to practice replacing them with feelings of hope and joy.

TASK: Make a list of ten times in your life where you created some outcome you were proud of and that increased the quality and functionality of your life. Take your time and think this through. Now, we invite you to read this list three times each day for the next thirty days to practice experiencing the feelings of pride. You solved a problem. You took on something new. You made something happen. As you get used to the feeling of pride, project that feeling forward. Imagine you are solving all of the problems you face. Allow yourself to experience joy and hope for your future.

EXERCISE 3B – SELF-DETERMINATION, ERODING

Exercise 3 invites you to begin taking control of your behavior in such a way that your self-determination expands. In Exercise 3 of Session 1, you discovered the amount of time that you have been wasting by being passive. You have been avoiding solving your own problems and creating positive things for your life, and instead have been drifting.

TASK: Take out your list from Exercise 3 of Session 1, and consider what constructive activities you can engage in during those times when you have been passive. If you have been playing video games, you might choose to take a walk as a first step to losing weight or getting into better physical shape. Create a plan for every block of time you have been wasting. Now, begin to put those plans into play.

EXERCISE 4B – SELF-DETERMINATION, ERODING

In Exercise 4 of Session 1, you faced bad habits that have been limiting your self-determination. These are patterns of behavior that become comfortable and may be difficult to break. In Exercise 4, we invite you to break those bad habits.

TASK: Get out your list. First, we want you prioritize them from the most detrimental to your functioning to the least detrimental. We want you to take on the most detrimental habit first because you will get the greatest gain for breaking this habit. Changing habits can be challenging because we become so used to them. The best approach is to substitute a more functional activity for a bad habit. For example, if you find yourself watching hours of television instead of finishing a work project because you think it is hopeless to try to advance your career, you might decide to take one hour every evening to focus on your work project before you turn on the television. You are creating a more helpful habit. So, decide what you will do in place of your most costly habit and begin doing it.

SESSION 3

EXERCISE 1C – SELF-DETERMINATION, ERODING

The focus of Session 3 is to prepare you to begin the process of taking control of the areas of your life you have abdicated responsibility.

Exercise 1 invites you to focus on identifying the issues that are most critical. This should be your starting point. In Session 2, you made lists of patterns of thinking, feeling, behavior, and habits that are undermining your well-being. Now, it is time to prioritize them.

TASK: Go back through your lists and pick the five that are currently most detrimental to your life. Be ruthless in your selection. Don't avoid ones that might be difficult if they are important. Now, take your list of five and prioritize them from the most impactful to the least impactful. Which one will provide you the most benefit when you change it? This one will be the focus of your work.

EXERCISE 2C – SELF-DETERMINATION, ERODING

Exercise 2 invites you to consider the resources available to you as you plan to take charge of the issue you identified in Exercise 1. This step is very important and is often overlooked. Resources are often people in your life who care about you, wish you well, and are willing to assist you if you ask for help. Resources can also be support groups, seminars, therapists, and coaches. One of the reasons people fail when they set out to make a change is because they lack adequate resources.

TASK: Making a list of resources may require doing some research. Talk to friends and family about resources of which they are aware. Check with your company to see if they make resources available to you. Determine which resources will be the most helpful and which you can afford.

EXERCISE 3C – SELF-DETERMINATION, ERODING

Exercise 3 invites you to identify obstacles that stand in the way of extending your self-determination into the area of your life you know needs to be changed. Identify internal resistance you may have. Write down every hesitancy you have about making this change. With every change there is a price to be paid, even with good ones.

TASK: Next, write down external obstacles. You might find that there are people in your life who don't want you to change. They might take comfort from the fact you are stuck in the same place they find themselves. Or, they might get some satisfaction from your failures. Finally, list any circumstances that might get in your way. Change often requires us to rearrange things in our lives; to change schedules, take on new disciplines, and to give up old habit patterns. Your list of obstacles is important because simply noticing them will make it easier for you to deal with them.

EXERCISE 4C – SELF-DETERMINATION, ERODING

Exercise 4 invites you to do the necessary internal work that precedes making a significant change. You must prepare yourself internally by thinking through the process you are planning to undertake. Write down the answers to the following questions: 1. Exactly what am I preparing to change? 2. Why am I making this change? 3. What will I have to give up to make this change? 4. How will I benefit from making this change? 5. Am I ready to do the work? This last question may be the most important. If you aren't ready, don't even start. You have already set yourself up for failure. It will be much better for you if you wait until you are ready.

TASK: Answering these questions will help you to marshal your internal resources as you see clearly where you are going and why you are going there.

SESSION 4
EXERCISE 1D – SELF-DETERMINATION, ERODING

Session 4 will guide you through the critical steps to regain control of areas of your life where you surrendered control to forces outside of yourself.

Exercise 1 invites you to set a clear goal. One of the major reasons people fail to control their lives is because they don't have clear goals. Imagine you were going on vacation with the only goal as "going west." While that sets a direction, it is too general to be very actionable. As a result, you are less likely to get started. You identified the most important area for you to change. Now, set a clear goal. We like to call this dreaming. Your goal doesn't have to be easy or practical. It does need to be exciting and useful. Your success won't be bigger than your goal, so dream big. What would excite you to achieve in this area of your life? What would make you feel very successful?

TASK: Write this down. This is your goal. Good work.

EXERCISE 2D – SELF-DETERMINATION, ERODING

Exercise 2 focuses your attention on creating a plan. Now that you know where you are headed, how will you get there? A plan breaks down a goal into clear and actionable steps. Without a good plan, your goal can feel overwhelming and impossible. Your plan will focus you on only the next step you need to take to move forward. That next step will seem much more possible to take and will keep you moving forward. Your plan should include: 1. A completion date. When do you plan to have achieved your goal? 2. Milestones. What are some miniature goals that move you toward a big goal? And, when do you plan to be at each one? 3. Action steps. What do you need to do every day to move you toward your milestones?

TASK: Write out your plan. Take your time and make it as complete as possible. Show your plan to someone who cares about you and ask for feedback. Revise it based on sound advice.

EXERCISE 3D – SELF-DETERMINATION, ERODING

Exercise 3 asks you to put your plan into action. Imagining change and planning are of little value if you don't put them to work. The most important step in change is the very first one. Most of the resistance to making changes happens before the first step. Once you take that step, the others will be easier. One of the best ways to encourage you to take the first step and then the next step is to be intentional. You become intentional by deciding when you are going to take each step and then putting those commitments in your calendar. Almost all successful people manage their time rather than allowing time to manage them. Your action steps should be of the highest priority. Decide the best time to do them; the time when you are least likely to be distracted by other things and when you will have the energy to act.

TASK: Write them in your calendar and guide your life by those commitments.

EXERCISE 4D – SELF-DETERMINATION, ERODING

Exercise 4 invites you to notice progress and make course corrections. Noticing progress is a great reinforcement for continuing to follow your plan. It should not take many action steps for you to begin to see the benefit of the changes you are making. It is that benefit that will encourage you to continue with your plan. Failure to take the time to notice progress or lack of appreciation of that success can greatly undermine your determination and follow through.

TASK: Keep a log of your successes and review them each day. No plan can anticipate how things will play out. Your plan should be a living document that can change and adjust as you learn new things. You may discover new obstacles or new resources that require some adaptation of your milestones and action steps. Don't hesitate to make these changes.

FACTOR – SELF-DETERMINATION

This factor focuses on the ability to think and act on behalf of yourself. It is not selfishness, but is the ability to balance your desires and goals with those of the broader community in such a way that you are able to continue to grow, develop, and be fully self-expressed. Self-Determined people are those who have the ability to lead others because they are not enmeshed in the neediness of dependency.

SELF-ASSESSED RATING – TREADING WATER

You determine most of the key aspects of your life but feel at the effect of areas necessary for greater growth.

SESSION 1

EXERCISE 1A – SELF-DETERMINATION, TREADING WATER

You are treading water in your life because you are not sufficiently exercising your self-determination. You are coasting instead of pushing forward toward building a life that is thriving. In Session 1, we invite you to consider how you are holding yourself back. Let's get started.

Exercise 1 asks you to focus on your thinking. Treading water is about accepting life as "good enough." We call this the "dead zone." When your life is "good enough," you tend to accept things as they are, to stop creating dreams for the future, and to make yourself content with the status quo.

TASK: Write down all of the ways you think your life is good enough. Perhaps it is eye-opening for you to see how you have made yourself content with your life as it is. Such thinking will not motivate you to reach for more.

EXERCISE 2A – SELF-DETERMINATION, TREADING WATER

Exercise 2 invites you to consider your emotions. Feelings can drive change or undermine it. The feeling often experienced by those who are treading water is contentment. There is little disturbance of either emotional pain or desire. Comfort is one of the feelings that erode self-determination. If life feels good enough, there is no need to work to create something different or more.

TASK: Write down how you feel about the following areas of your life: 1. Intimate relationship, 2. Family, 3. Career, 4. Physical condition, 5. Interests and hobbies, 6. Meaning and purpose. Do you notice much desire or frustration? If not, can you feel the lethargy that comes from being content with things as they are?

EXERCISE 3A – SELF-DETERMINATION, TREADING WATER

Exercise 3 invites you to take a look at how you have been behaving. If you are treading water, it is likely that you are coasting. You are doing enough to maintain your life but not exerting much, if any, energy or effort toward advancing. Advancing is almost more difficult than maintaining. Advancing requires having a vision of where you want to go, letting go of comfortable habits, and taking on new skills and behavior. It is very important that you do an honest assessment of how you are behaving, because actions do speak louder than words. You may be fooling yourself with talk about changes you want to make while, in fact, your behavior suggests you aren't making any changes at all.

TASK: List all of the ways you are coasting. Take a look at the list. Are you content with the choices you have been making?

EXERCISE 4A – SELF-DETERMINATION, TREADING WATER

Exercise 4 invites you to focus on habit patterns you have developed. Habits are simply behaviors that become routine. Habits can be helpful when they propel us to make necessary changes. Habits can be harmful when they lull us into a sense of calm and acceptance such that we accept what is good instead of striving for what is best. It is likely that you don't have many very bad habits or your life would be declining. But, it is also likely that you need to cultivate new habits that rouse you from your slumber and press you to take on greater challenges and needed changes.

TASK: Make a list of the habits that are undermining your life and those that are helping. Which list is longer? Are you content with your habits as they are?

SESSION 2

EXERCISE 1B – SELF-DETERMINATION, TREADING WATER

Session 2 encourages you to prepare yourself for the changes you need to make to move toward thriving. Let's get started.

Exercise 1 invites you to shift your thinking from "this is enough" to "there is more." One powerful way to do this is to imagine your life five years and then ten years from now. If nothing changed in your life, would you be content? If you were doing the same thing as you are doing now, living just as you are now living, would you be content? What more do you want for your life? This is such an important question because the answer largely determines the outcome. Everything you create in your life started with a desire to want it. Hence, your dreams and goals have creative power. Now is your time to get creative. If you don't want to be where you are now ten years from now, what do you want that you don't have?

TASK: Write it all down. Have fun. Be bold.

EXERCISE 2B – SELF-DETERMINATION, TREADING WATER

Exercise 2 asks you to focus on your feelings. You may have been surprised by how content you felt about your life. You have done a good job and created some comfort for yourself. You are reasonably successful. You don't live with much worry about the future. But, for you to thrive, you must cultivate the feeling of excitement. Excitement can motivate great change. Excitement comes from imagining what might be and believing it is possible to have it. The clearer you are about your desires and the more you believe they can be yours, the greater your excitement will be.

TASK: Take out your list from Session 1. As you read each desire, give yourself the time and create the room to feel excited. Let it build. Imagine you had the thing that you longed for. Let this emotion begin to propel you forward.

EXERCISE 3B – SELF-DETERMINATION, TREADING WATER

Exercise 3 invites you to focus on your behaviors. You may have noticed that much of your behavior was coasting; only maintaining what you already have. You are doing little to move forward. You aren't taking any courses, investing in any new hobbies, making many new friends, or preparing for many changes. You have grown used to being static instead of being in motion. The more you train yourself to be in motion, the more natural motion will be. Instead of coasting, you can train yourself to always be moving forward in some way or other.

TASK: Make a list of some things you can begin doing that move you forward in some way. You don't have to start big. Simply pick one and put in it play. That one change will make it easier for you to get in action in other areas of your life.

EXERCISE 4B – SELF-DETERMINATION, TREADING WATER

Exercise 4 invites you to focus on your habits. You have seen that you have some habit patterns that encourage you to maintain the status quo. They aren't bad habits that undermine your improvement. But, they aren't good habits that require that you are always moving forward. You should learn to cultivate habits that support continued growth. They might include reading books, visiting museums, traveling, having stimulating conversations with friends, eating in different restaurants, taking courses, or engaging a coach. All of these activities and many more will encourage you to think new thoughts, dream new dreams, and cultivate new opportunities.

TASK: Make a list of expanding activities that could become habits for you. Now decide how much time each week you will spend on those activities. Be generous. Invest in yourself.

SESSION 3

EXERCISE 1C – SELF-DETERMINATION, TREADING WATER

Session 3 focuses on actions you can take that will increase your self-determination.

Exercise 1 encourages you to expand your dream for your life. Almost everyone dreams too small. We see our limitations far more clearly than we see what is amazing and wonderful. And, since our dreams control the greatness of our life, it is only when we see who we truly can become that our dreams will be supportive of our greatness. So, we are asking you to get in touch with your greatness to the best of your ability. Perhaps you have encountered your greatness in your love for your children. You instinctively tune into their needs and feed their greatness. Or, you may have discovered your greatness in your work. You seem to know what to do as if you were born with those insights. Most of us have stumbled across our greatness from time to time. Now, you need to tune into it and imagine how big and amazing it could be.

TASK: Take some time and write down when you have found your greatness and what you think it could be and do.

EXERCISE 2C – SELF-DETERMINATION, TREADING WATER

In Exercise 2 we invite you to feed your ambition. It is more than okay to want more. In fact, we should all want more all of the time. Wanting more fuels change. One of the problems with wanting more is that we judge ourselves as if it isn't okay to have unbridled ambition or we are shamed by others for our desires. We encourage you to throw off those constraints and to want more without any judgment. Simply notice what you want and accept it.

TASK: Write down whatever comes to mind and welcome it as your friend. Enjoy your ambition; it is the fuel in your engine that will carry you to great things. Review this list every day for the next week and write down whatever comes to mind. Don't hold back.

EXERCISE 3C – SELF-DETERMINATION, TREADING WATER

Exercise 3 invites you to commit to always be improving. Your life is a piece of artwork that is never finished. Regardless of how well you have done, how comfortable you are, and what you have accomplished, there is always room for you to improve. The most meaningful goal in life is to keep polishing and cultivating our "being" such that our lives are bigger, wiser, more balanced, and more meaningful. The work we can do on ourselves is never done. When we stop moving forward, we cheat ourselves of the life we could have and of the person we could be. We invite you to get used to the commitment to take on the next phase of your growth and development. This week we want you to consider all of the opportunities available to you to grow and expand your "being." What feeds your soul? Who challenges you to have a bigger perspective?

TASK: Make a list and commit to engaging in at least one thing that will keep you moving toward the person you could be.

EXERCISE 4C – SELF-DETERMINATION, TREADING WATER

Exercise 4 invites you to consider the meaning of your life and how it can expand. We all start out our lives with very self-centered goals. Our lives are about ourselves. As we mature, we find greater meaning by taking on responsibility for the welfare of others—our friends, our spouse, our children, and our community. Subordinating your self-interest for the interest of others gives your life greater richness and depth. And, you don't need to stop there. When you take on causes that impact the welfare of others, even those you don't know, your sense of meaning and purpose continue to expand. This is one of the best ways to move toward thriving.

TASK: Make a list of causes that matter to you or people who need your encouragement and support. Choose to invest in something that takes you out of your comfort zone and away from focusing on yourself, so as to bring greater purpose and meaning to your life.

SESSION 4
EXERCISE 1D – SELF-DETERMINATION, TREADING WATER

Session 4 is designed to help you become more comfortable with the change necessary to move out of treading water and toward growing.

Exercise 1 asks you to focus on giving up comfort. There is certainly nothing wrong with being comfortable. Comfort is something we all seek. But, comfort is meant to be a resting place to regroup while we prepare for the next phase of our journey. When comfort becomes our home from which we are unwilling to leave, it becomes an obstacle to growth and change. We invite you to pay attention to the comfort you now enjoy.

TASK: Write down everything you like about your current life. Take time to appreciate everything that is wonderful about it. Now, consider saying goodbye to your comfort as you welcome your new life challenge. It is very useful to grow accustomed to letting go of our comfort for the next adventure. Practice with little things, like uncluttering to make room for new things. Give up some old habit for a new one. Make a new friend. Keep looking for ways to introduce new opportunities into your life.

EXERCISE 2D – SELF-DETERMINATION, TREADING WATER

Exercise 2 invites you to look for new territory to expand and grow. We all grow accustomed to our friends, habits, patterns, and routines. The more accustomed we become, the more difficult it can be to take on something new or to explore someplace unfamiliar. Limiting our experience limits our possibilities and so narrows our life focus.

TASK: This week we want you to consider expanding into new, uncharted, unfamiliar, and unexpected territories for your life. Think of things that are out of character for you. You might choose to learn a new language, vacation in a foreign country, build a friendship with someone from a different race or background, and learn to cook a new cuisine. These are opportunities to get out of your comfort zone and take on something unexpected. Amazing things can happen when we enter unknown spaces and take on uncharacteristic challenges. Become an explorer.

EXERCISE 3D – SELF-DETERMINATION, TREADING WATER

Advancing your self-determination requires developing an acceptance of change. Exercise 3 invites you to welcome change into your life and to use change to cultivate positive growth. Most people resist change because of a bias to think that things are as good as they can be and that change will only mess up what is working. In truth, the opposite is more often the case. Change is often more positive than negative. We hold ourselves back by resisting the very changes we need. Consider your childhood. It was filled with change for which you were quite eager. You weren't content to lie still. You wanted to crawl. You weren't content to crawl. You wanted to walk. This early pattern is something we need as adults. To get comfortable with change, make a list of some of the big changes you have made in your life. Did they turn out for the better or for the worse? If for the better, shouldn't you be seeking changes?

TASK: Begin looking for and welcoming change into your life, both big and small.

EXERCISE 4D – SELF-DETERMINATION, TREADING WATER

Exercise 4 invites you to a life that is in constant motion. In truth, there is simply too much to do to sit by and coast. There is too much to learn, to explore, to taste, and to try. When we are coasting in comfort, we are missing out on all there is to discover in the fascinating life we have been given. In many ways, it almost doesn't matter what you try as long as you try something new. It doesn't matter where you go as long as you go somewhere. Being in motion creates its own path and opens up new opportunities. We want you to become uncomfortable with every routine, viewing each of them as an enticement to avoid the adventure you are meant to have.

TASK: Make a list of all of your comfortable habits. Now, make a list of as many new adventures as you can imagine. Get off the coach and start experimenting.

FACTOR – SELF-DETERMINATION

This factor focuses on the ability to think and act on behalf of yourself. It is not selfishness, but the ability to balance your desires and goals with those of the broader community in such a way that you are able to continue to grow, develop, and be fully self-expressed. Self-determined people are those who have the ability to lead others because they are not enmeshed in the neediness of dependency.

SELF-ASSESSED RATING – GROWING

You determine almost every aspect of your life. There are only one or two areas where you aren't in control.

SESSION 1

EXERCISE 1A – SELF-DETERMINATION, GROWING

You are growing because you have, for the most part, exercised self-determination to manage your life. You know how to think and act on your own behalf to keep making your life better. But if you aren't fully thriving, it is likely that you have one or two areas of your life where you have abdicated responsibility and, for some reason, are not taking charge. Session 1 is designed to assist you in understanding the experience of less than complete self-determination. Let's get started.

Exercise 1 asks you to consider how you think when you are allowing one or two issues to stand in your way. It is likely that whatever those one or two issues are, they are so important to you that you are unwilling to address them openly and honestly. You might be living with someone you don't deeply love, toward whom you are harboring some resentment or who has some destructive habit like an addiction. You know something is wrong, but you don't want to face the conflict and/or fear the consequence of doing so. You can recognize this thinking pattern when you know you are settling for some situation that you don't fully like.

TASK: Make a list of any issues that came to mind while you were reading this. Write down all of your concerns with regard to dealing with these issues.

EXERCISE 2A – SELF-DETERMINATION, GROWING

Exercise 2 invites you to consider the feelings that are associated with holding back on your self-determination. Because you know what it looks like to manage your own life, it is likely that you experience periodic frustration and irritation toward the person or situation that you are allowing to hold you back from fully thriving. It isn't a constant irritant because you have a pretty functional life that provides you with meaning and satisfaction. But, with some regularity, you bump into this situation or person and keep having the same experience of not liking what happens to you in those encounters. You might feel held back in some way or as if you are being pressured into going along with things that you know aren't the best for you or for the situation. Pay attention to these feelings. They will guide you toward the resolution of this situation.

TASK: Make a list of all of the times in the past week when you have experienced the emotions just discussed. What issues triggered those emotions?

EXERCISE 3A – SELF-DETERMINATION, GROWING

Exercise 3 asks you to consider your behavior in relation to the one or two issues that you are allowing to hold your life back. Typically, you will find yourself trying to avoid encounters with the person(s) or situations that are less than fully functional or don't enhance your life. You don't enjoy experiencing those situations and try to minimize their impact on your life. You aren't yet willing to address them and so know they won't go away. You are hoping they will solve themselves and find yourself putting up with and enduring circumstances you don't like.

TASK: Keep a journal this week and notice every circumstance or person you find yourself seeking to avoid. These might be obvious or subtle. You might find yourself pretending to read to avoid a conversation. Or, you might duck into a cubicle to avoid talking to someone. Every time you find yourself avoiding, you should know that you are choosing to turn away from something you need to confront if you are to fully thrive.

EXERCISE 4A – SELF-DETERMINATION, GROWING

Exercise 4 invites you to consider the habit patterns you have developed. Habits are simply complex behaviors to which we have grown accustomed and that allow us to efficiently deal with our life circumstances. Some habits are very helpful. Others get in the way of our growth and development. You have chosen to tolerate one or two issues that you know should be resolved but seem too risky to take on. If you are attentive, you will discover that you have cultivated some habits that deaden you to the price you are paying to sacrifice your self-determination. You might have created a habit of snacking when you are with this person you are tolerating. Somehow, eating lessens your tension or compensates for your frustration. You could start drinking in the evening to quiet your anxiety about issues you are avoiding at work. Such habits make it more difficult to feel the negative emotions that might actually lead to constructive change.

TASK: Make a list of habits you have developed that allow you to tolerate rather than deal with the issues in your life.

SESSION 2

EXERCISE 1B – SELF-DETERMINATION, GROWING

Session 2 invites you to begin shifting the patterns identified in Session 1 in a manner that will prepare you to take on the issues you have been avoiding. Let's get started.

Exercise 1 addresses your thinking patterns. You discovered that you have some "sacred cows," issues or people you don't want to deal with because you think the consequences of doing so might be too costly or messy. This way of thinking makes complete sense until you consider the price you are paying to maintain the status quo. You are actually sacrificing your life because you fear the cost of change. This is a common barrier for many people. But, all who thrive have been here many times and have pushed through these barriers. You must value your life more highly than any other circumstance or person. You can only control your life.

TASK: Make a list of who you could be and what you might do if you took control of the one or two issues you have been avoiding.

EXERCISE 2B – SELF-DETERMINATION, GROWING

Exercise 2 asks you to begin to shift your feelings from frustration and irritation to excitement fueled by the vision of your life without the burden of this one unresolved issue. Your current feelings are based on you being stuck in your current situation. But, as you expand your self-determination, you will liberate yourself from the entanglement that has been holding you back and will be free to enjoy more of your potential. The more you allow yourself to be filled up with the excitement of where you are going, the more energy and focus you will have to break through the barriers that you have allowed to hold you back. We invite you to do a visioning exercise.

TASK: Write down how your life will look when you have broken through. Now, close your eyes and focus on the details of that vision. Try it for 5-10 minutes each day for the next week. Let your life be filled with the positive energy of excitement.

EXERCISE 3B – SELF-DETERMINATION, GROWING

Exercise 3 invites you to shift your behavior from managing and avoiding your circumstances to confronting the issues directly and completely. The goal here is to rid yourself of all negative energy in your life. Whatever you are avoiding needs to be addressed.

TASK: Make a list of the people you have not been fully candid with. What message do you need to deliver to them? Make a list of any circumstances that need to be changed. What changes need to be made to bring your life into full alignment? These two lists will create clear goals for the changes you need to make.

Resist avoiding any issue in your life. Pay attention to the moment you begin to turn away and turn toward it instead.

EXERCISE 4B – SELF-DETERMINATION, GROWING

Exercise 4 invites you to begin to alter the habit patterns in your life. Your habits have supported you in avoiding some important issues. They have compensated for your frustration and irritation. They must now be replaced with habits that support continuous improvement regardless of the obstacles you face. Such habits are supported by friends who are constantly improving their lives. They are fostered by commitments you make to getting an advanced degree, mastering a musical instrument, or learning a cooking technique. Everything that requires new learning and forces you to confront the unknown is helpful in building the habits of continuous improvement.

TASK: Make a list of three things you are willing to take on that will help you forge the habit of continuously improving your life.

SESSION 3
EXERCISE 1C – SELF-DETERMINATION, GROWING

Session 3 will focus on specific obstacles to the changes you need to make. Understanding obstacles is often a necessary first step toward making positive change. Let's get started.

The first obstacle is lethargy. We all grow accustomed to our circumstances, even those that aren't optimal. The first step of change is often the most difficult because we must break free of the tendency to perpetuate whatever is occurring. Change isn't cheap. There are almost always consequences for changing. One way to deal with apathy is to imagine you do nothing to change your situation. Your life isn't bad, but it isn't great. Can you accept being in the same circumstance five or ten years from now? If that thought makes you uneasy, you know you need to make some change.

TASK: Pay attention to your level of conviction. You may or may not be ready to begin the change process now. If not, that is okay. Wait until your motivation to change is greater than your apathy.

EXERCISE 2C – SELF-DETERMINATION, GROWING

Exercise 2 invites you to focus on relational obstacles. While you are likely supported by many people who wish the best for you, it might also be true that you have a few people in your life who envy your success and who unconsciously or consciously will try to sabotage your efforts to break free of these final one or two entanglements. It is important to not be naive lest you depend on people who don't have your best interest in mind.

TASK: Make a list of the people you can count on to push you and to encourage your forward progress. Now, make a list of the people you aren't sure you can trust or know you can't trust. Use these two lists to build your support network. Make sure you aren't confiding in or trusting those you aren't certain you can count on.

EXERCISE 3C – SELF-DETERMINATION, GROWING

Exercise 3 invites you to consider circumstantial obstacles. You might be going through a stressful time at work that is draining your energy to take on an important issue in your family. Or, you may have health issues that should be resolved before you sign up to make a major change in your career. On the other hand, you might now be in a place where you have a great deal of support from those around you and life is providing a clear opportunity to change. Your boss may be considering promoting a few people into key roles just at the time when you know you need to make a job change. Or, the last argument with your spouse made it clear that the two of you weren't meant to live together.

TASK: It is wise to make two lists. The first should list all of the external resources available to support making a change. The other should include all of the external issues that drain your attention and energy. Use these lists to decide if this is the right time to make a big shift.

EXERCISE 4C – SELF-DETERMINATION, GROWING

Exercise 4 focuses on your emotional state. Change can require significant emotional, mental, and physical energy. Are you currently in a place where your internal resources are high or low? Change is sometimes fueled by difficulty and pain. We simply can't tolerate the status quo any longer. A better alternative is when change is fueled by vision and desire. When you can see what you want and don't have, you are better able to marshal positive energy like desire, excitement, and joy.

TASK: Make a list of some new habits you can create that will support the changes you want to make. These can include anything that prepares you for the outcome you want to create. You might begin reading topics that will lead to a new job or learn a new skill that will transfer to your workplace.

SESSION 4
EXERCISE 1D – SELF-DETERMINATION, GROWING

Session 4 will assist you in making concrete and lasting change.

Exercise 1 invites you to focus on the most immediate obstacle you face in your path toward thriving. While you might immediately think of many things, there is actually only one immediate obstacle. If you were traveling down a road and were blocked by a fallen tree, there might be many obstacles in your path farther down the road but the tree in front of you is your immediate one. You can move no further until you deal with it.

TASK: Write it down. Write why it is an obstacle and how it is blocking your path. Get very clear, because you will now be moving it out of your way. Don't let your mind wander to how or the cost of moving it. Stay focused on that one thing and how it is holding you back.

EXERCISE 2D – SELF-DETERMINATION, GROWING

Exercise 2 invites you to take stock of the cost of living with this obstacle. It has been blocking your path and you have been paying a price for not dealing with it. That price might include missed opportunities, frustration, wasted time, limitations in taking on new things, financial loss, loss of friendships, and many other things. Take a complete stock of everything you have lost as a result of not solving this problem.

TASK: Write them down. Realize that you will soon stop all of these losses by dealing directly with this issue. All of this pain will go away. You will finally be free to pursue your life with zeal and determination.

EXERCISE 3D – SELF-DETERMINATION, GROWING

Exercise 3 is time to get clear about what exactly you need to do to deal with the issue that is standing in your way. Every problem has a solution. Every obstacle has a way to move or get around it. You may need to be creative, persistent, brave, and fearless. But in the end, it will be worth the effort and sacrifice for you to clear your path to move on.

TASK: Before you take action, create a plan. What conversation do you need to have that you have been avoiding? What action do you know you need to take that you have been unwilling to take until today? Get very clear. When will you have this conversation and/or take this action? What do you need to support your action plan? Create your plan and be specific. The clearer you are, the easier it will be to act.

EXERCISE 4D – SELF-DETERMINATION, GROWING

Exercise 4 is the final step. It is time to put your plan into action. You may need the support of friends to deal with this issue. Tell your network of trusted people what you intend to do, when you are doing it, and the reason you are taking action. Ask them to hold you accountable to execute on your plan. Don't overthink the situation. Just act. The more you anticipate how things will go, the more likely you will talk yourself out of moving forward. Trust that you are adequate to deal with whatever occurs. Be fearless in siding with your life and doing what is best for you. Trust that your courage and action will be rewarded with opportunity and growth. You will flourish and your life will become a greater resource to share with others. Investing in your life is an investment in the world. The greater you become, the more you have to share.

TASK: Now, do it!

EXERCISE SERIES:
SELF-EFFICACY

FACTOR – SELF-EFFICACY

This factor refers to your confidence in your ability to exert control over your own motivation, behavior, and social environment. People who have high self-efficacy see themselves as capable of shaping their world to suit themselves. Those who have low self-efficacy feel at the effect of the world around them.

SELF-ASSESSED RATING – HANGING ON

You completely lack confidence in your ability to take control of your life and to craft it to suit you.

SESSION 1

EXERCISE 1A – SELF-EFFICACY, HANGING ON

You are hanging on by your fingernails in life, partly because you almost completely lack confidence in your ability to exert control over your own motivation, behavior, and social environment. You may have grown accustomed to living this way and don't see how it is undermining your success and happiness. Session 1 is designed to open your eyes such that you clearly see what needs to be changed.

Exercise 1 invites you to focus on your level of motivation to change. It is likely that you have fallen into the feeling that any effort to try to change is useless because you don't believe it will accomplish anything good. Perhaps you have gone through a tough time or you have experienced a series of failures. Events such as these can erode confidence and motivation.

TASK: Make a list of all of the circumstances that might currently be undermining your motivation to believe that you can change. Simply writing these down can reduce the impact they have on holding you back.

EXERCISE 2A – SELF-EFFICACY, HANGING ON

Exercise 2 asks you to focus on your behavior; notice the choices you are making and what your behavior says about your confidence in your ability to control your world. Clearly, some choices we make are offensive. They are designed to make things happen and to advance our lives. Others are defensive. They are designed to protect and secure us when we are in tough situations. Other choices indicate we have surrendered, as if there is nothing we can do to help ourselves. Draw three columns and label them "offensive," "defensive," and "surrender."

TASK: List under each column choices that you are making or have made with regard to your life. Which list is longer?

EXERCISE 3A – SELF-EFFICACY, HANGING ON

Exercise 3 invites you to consider the people with whom you have chosen to relate and how they impact your confidence in your ability to control your life. The people in your life either support your efforts to make your life better or they conspire to undermine your confidence by making excuses for your inability to manage your life effectively and/or blaming life's circumstances as being too much for you to handle. The messages you receive from your friends and family are very powerful in shaping your confidence.

TASK: Make two lists; one of friends and family who support your growth and success and the second of those who make excuses for your lack of effective living. As you move forward in these exercises, you may need to change the balance of these two lists.

EXERCISE 4A – SELF-EFFICACY, HANGING ON

Exercise 4 invites you to consider the circumstances of your life. It is certainly true that some people seem to be blessed with good circumstances that appear to make it easy for them to succeed and thrive, while others appear to have more difficult and challenging circumstances. It is likely that you view yourself in the second group. Regardless, in truth, the most valuable skill to have in life is to have the confidence to take whatever is positive in your circumstances and to leverage that into something better. We will expand on that skill in later exercises. Right now, we want you to become aware of how you view your circumstances.

TASK: Make two columns; one for positive circumstances and the other for negative circumstances. List whatever comes to mind in the appropriate column. It is likely you view most, if not all, of your circumstances as negative.

SESSION 2

EXERCISE 1B – SELF-EFFICACY, HANGING ON

The key to forward momentum in your life is your degree of confidence. Without confidence, you lack the key ingredient to shape your world. In Session 2 we focus your attention on different aspects of self-confidence and ask you to assess yourself on each. Each one is important for you to understand, and eventually to master, if you are to move forward in your life.

Exercise 1 invites you to consider your confidence in your ability to set goals. Setting goals is the first step in change because it requires you to envision a preferred condition. In order to set goals, you must have confidence that you can actually have a better life.

TASK: Rate your confidence in your ability to create a better life on a scale from 1 (completely confident) to 10 (no confidence). Then write down the reason you gave yourself that rating.

EXERCISE 2B – SELF-EFFICACY, HANGING ON

Exercise 2 invites you to consider your level of confidence in your ability to create effective plans. Goals are of no value until you can create the pathway to accomplish them. You might want to get to the top of the mountain, but until you can see your path up it, it will seem impossible to reach the top. You may have had big goals for yourself at some point in your life but were never able to achieve them. In the process, you lost confidence in your ability to make good things happen for yourself.

TASK: Rate your ability to make effective plans from 1 (completely confident) to 10 (no confidence). Then write down the reason you gave yourself that rating.

EXERCISE 3B – SELF-EFFICACY, HANGING ON

Exercise 3 invites you to consider your level of confidence in your ability to make the right choices. You may have proven to yourself that you can set useful goals and even create quality plans. But, for some reason, you lacked the self-discipline to follow through. You may have little or no confidence that you can execute even the smallest and most beneficial plans for your life.

TASK: Rate your ability to make the right choices for yourself from 1 (completely confident) to 10 (no confidence). Then write down the reason you gave yourself that score.

EXERCISE 4B – SELF-EFFICACY, HANGING ON

Exercise 4 invites you to consider your level of confidence to persevere. Even if you set goals, make effective plans, and make the right choice, it is only when you can hold that course and continue down that path that you will gain the reward of your effort in positive life change. You may have found yourself frequently distracted or simply lacking the ability to keep yourself engaged in the plan you know would be helpful for you to achieve. Perhaps you started many great diet plans but never completed any. Or, you sent out a bunch of résumés but never followed through on the interviews. In the process, you have damaged your confidence in your ability to effectively follow through. Your lack of confidence now interferes with your ability to start anything new.

TASK: Rate your confidence in your ability to follow through from 1 (completely confident) to 10 (no confidence). Then write down the reasons you gave yourself that score.

SESSION 3

EXERCISE 1C – SELF-EFFICACY, HANGING ON

Session 3 invites you to begin to shift from having little or no confidence in your ability to shape your life in a positive way to believing that you can. Belief is the foundation of all successful action. You simply must believe. Let's get started.

Exercise 1 invites you to cultivate belief that life is your friend, that it holds many positive possibilities for your life. This may be challenging, since your past might tell a different story. But, perhaps some of your past negative experiences were due to the fact that you didn't believe that life was your ally. In order to begin to gain confidence in your partnership with life, we invite you to take notice of all that life has provided for you and all of the ways it has supported you, rather than focusing on what didn't work out well.

TASK: Please make a list of all that life has provided for you in order to have a successful and powerful life. Be thoughtful. Consider the country in which you were born, and the gifts and skills with which you were endowed. Add to this list every day and open yourself to a stronger belief in your ability to partner with life in a positive manner.

EXERCISE 2C – SELF-EFFICACY, HANGING ON

Exercise 2 invites you to shift from having little or no confidence in your ability to create a meaningful life to gaining some confidence in yourself. It is likely that you have a clear understanding of the mistakes you have made and the choices that didn't work out. You may have a litany of dreams that didn't come true and of circumstances that have made life harder for you. But, you may not be seeing clearly how you have actively shaped your life for good. You may have overlooked times when you created success and when you used your gifts and abilities to make good things happen. It is critical that you are able to see your ability to make your life better. Your confidence rests on that foundation.

TASK: Make a list of all of the successes you have created for yourself. Be thoughtful and take your time. None is too small to add to the list. Don't even consider your failures and problems. Notice that you have been effective more often than you realized. You need to begin to see yourself as someone who has the ability to shape life in your best interest.

EXERCISE 3C – SELF-EFFICACY, HANGING ON

Exercise 3 invites you to shift from having little or no confidence in your ability to effectively work with others to make positive things happen to believing in your skill to interact with the people in your life effectively and positively. While you might not always see it, if you are willing, you will notice that you have had a positive impact on many people in your life and many people have had a positive influence on yours. You have formed alliances with people in the past that have worked out well for everyone and that have shaped their life and yours in a positive way. You may have partnered with someone to raise a family and can see how your children have been blessed by your commitment to them. You may have friends you reached out and supported when they were going through a hard time and who are on solid footing because of you. You may have had friends who encouraged you to believe in yourself and because of whom you achieved something important to you. Every one of those partnerships proves that you can make a difference in the lives of others and can invite others to make a difference in your own.

TASK: Make a list of all of those relationships that have worked out well. Noticing the positive impact you have can begin to restore your confidence in yourself.

EXERCISE 4C – SELF-EFFICACY, HANGING ON

Exercise 4 invites you to shift from having little or no confidence in your ability to manage your circumstances to believing in your skill to make things better regardless of what life throws at you. It would be wonderful if life only provided you with abundant opportunities that required little effort or resourcefulness on your part. But rarely, if ever, does that occur. It is crucial that you come to believe that you can control your circumstances, even when things are hard and your options are limited. In his classic book *Man's Search for Meaning*, Viktor Frankl pointed out that one of the fundamental building blocks of survival and thriving is to work with whatever control is available to you regardless of the circumstances. It is learning to see past the obstacles in order to see the opportunities and to leverage those to make things better. It is likely that you have done exactly that more often than you have noticed. You have found yourself in hard times and found a way to get through.

TASK: Make a list of some of the difficulties you have overcome in your life. Now, write down what opportunities you discovered in each one that allowed you to get through it. Seeing your resourcefulness is encouragement to believe you possess this skill and can continue to improve it.

SESSION 4
EXERCISE 1D – SELF-EFFICACY, HANGING ON

Session 4 will provide you with some basic, but important, skills to build on your foundation of confidence that you can, in fact, shape your world for the better.

Exercise 1 asks you to begin cultivating the skill of vision. Vision is built on the idea that you must envision what you want before you can make it happen. You aren't likely to lose weight until you can envision yourself thinner. You aren't likely to make much more money until you can envision your life with more money. Visioning requires increasing your confidence in yourself. You need to believe that your dreams can come true. If you don't believe, you won't dream or you will dream small.

TASK: Practice writing down a few things you want to make your life better. It doesn't matter at this point if they are ambitious or not. It is only important that you want them. Review your list every day this week and ask yourself if you believe you can actually make these things happen. Cross out those in which you don't believe. If you have only one that remains, that is enough.

EXERCISE 2D – SELF-EFFICACY, HANGING ON

Exercise 2 invites you to begin cultivating confidence in your ability to thoughtfully and meaningfully plan. Change doesn't happen simply because you want something that you don't have. It doesn't have a chance of happening until you plan the pathway to make it happen. Plans break down a vision into small enough steps to be practical. Those steps must take into account your resources, skills, determination, obstacles, and perseverance. A plan that is too ambitious can set you up for certain failure. A plan that takes too long can be discouraging. A plan that requires resources that aren't available to you isn't practical. In order for you to gain confidence in your ability to successfully craft your life, you must have growing confidence in your ability to effectively plan.

TASK: Take one of the visions you listed in Exercise 1. Create a plan. Notice where you are having difficulties or setting yourself up for problems. Keep working on it until you can sit back, review it, and believe that you have what it takes to actually execute on it.

EXERCISE 3D – SELF-EFFICACY, HANGING ON

Exercise 3 invites you to begin cultivating confidence that you can actually follow through on your plans to the very end. If the journey toward your goals is abandoned, it fails to achieve the outcome you desired and becomes a discouragement for every future effort. On the other hand, completing what you have started and reaping the benefit of your effort is encouragement to take on another goal. Every time you set a vision, create a plan, and successfully execute it, your confidence in your ability to constructively shape your life will grow stronger. Hence, it is very important to start small and to create a series of successes. Working on your plan will require a lot of you. You will need to stay focused, learn to delay gratification, discipline yourself, and follow through to the very end. These are not skills that everyone has developed. Starting small will allow you to practice and master each one.

TASK: Take out your plan from the last session and begin putting it into practice. Notice what comes easy to you. Notice what does not. Keep focused on the outcome at the end of the plan and use it to encourage yourself to keep going.

Make sure you succeed, because the outcome will be the natural expansion of your confidence.

EXERCISE 4D – SELF-EFFICACY, HANGING ON

Exercise 4 invites you to expand your self-confidence by celebrating, resting, reviewing, renewing, and expanding. When you achieve a goal that you set for yourself, be it big or small, it is reason to celebrate. Celebrations don't need to be wild and expensive. They can be as small as taking 30 minutes to appreciate yourself for the work you have done on your life. Celebrations help to break up the tasks of life into more bite-sized chunks. Next, rest.

TASK: Take a few days off. Don't take on your next vision until you have rested and renewed yourself. Use your rest time to review all that you learned on your journey. Write down what you learned about yourself, especially those things that you value and appreciate. Noticing your strengths and new skills will expand your resources for the next vision you take on and your confidence in yourself will grow. Now, when you are ready, take on your next project to make your life even better.

FACTOR – SELF-EFFICACY

This factor refers to your confidence in your ability to exert control over your own motivation, behavior, and social environment. People who have high self-efficacy see themselves as capable of shaping their world to suit themselves. Those who have low self-efficacy feel at the effect of the world around them.

SELF-ASSESSED RATING – ERODING

You are progressively losing confidence in your ability to control your life and to craft it to suit you.

SESSION 1

EXERCISE 1A – SELF-EFFICACY, ERODING

You are eroding in life, partly because you have diminishing confidence in your ability to exert control over your own motivation, behavior, and social environment. You are growing accustomed to living this way, and while you may see how it is undermining your success and happiness, you have not developed effective strategies to stop your downward slide and to move in a positive direction. Session 1 is designed to help you understand exactly why your confidence is in decline so you can prepare to change. Let's get started.

Exercise 1 invites you to focus on your level of motivation to change. You are watching the quality of your life slowly slip through your fingers, but that doesn't mean that you are motivated to make positive change. To the extent you are losing confidence in your ability to master your life circumstances, you are likely sliding into a sense of helplessness, as if there is nothing you can do to help yourself.

TASK: Please make a list of the issues that are supporting and those that are eroding your motivation to make the changes you know you must make.

EXERCISE 2A – SELF-EFFICACY, ERODING

Exercise 2 invites you to focus on your behavior; notice the choices you are making and what your behavior says about your confidence in your ability to control your world. Clearly, some choices we make are offensive. They are designed to make things happen and to advance our lives. Others are defensive. They are designed to protect and secure us when we are in tough situations. Other choices indicate we are surrendering control, as if we are losing confidence that we can help ourselves.

TASK: Draw three columns and label them "offensive," "defensive," and "surrender." List under each column choices that you are making or have made with regard to your life. Which list is longer? Do you notice that one of the three lists has been growing?

EXERCISE 3A – SELF-EFFICACY, ERODING

Exercise 3 invites you to consider the people with whom you have chosen to relate and their impact on your confidence in your ability to control your life. The people in your life either support your efforts to make your life better or they conspire to undermine your confidence by making excuses for your inability to manage your life effectively and/or blaming life's circumstances as being too much for you to handle. The messages you receive from your friends and family are very powerful in shaping your confidence.

TASK: Make two lists; one of friends and family who support your growth and success and the second of those who make excuses for your lack of effective living. As you move forward in these exercises, you may need to change the balance of these two lists. Have your seen a shift in the number of names in each list? Are you adding more people who are actually undermining your self-confidence?

EXERCISE 4A – SELF-EFFICACY, ERODING

Exercise 4 invites you to consider the circumstances of your life. It is certainly true that some people seem to be blessed with good circumstances that appear to make it easy for them to succeed and thrive, while others appear to have more difficult and challenging circumstances. It is likely that you view yourself as moving into the second group. Regardless, in truth, the most valuable skill to have in life is to have the confidence to take whatever is positive in your circumstances and to leverage that into something better. We will expand on that skill in later exercises. Right now, we want you to become aware of how you view your circumstances.

TASK: Make two columns; one for positive circumstances and the other for negative circumstances. List whatever comes to mind in the appropriate column. It is likely you view your circumstances as having been negative and continuing to be so. You are seeing the obstacles more clearly than the possibilities.

SESSION 2
EXERCISE 1B – SELF-EFFICACY, ERODING

The key to forward momentum in your life is your degree of confidence. By increasing your confidence you are gaining the key ingredient to shape your world. In Session 2 we focus your attention on different aspects of self-confidence and ask you to assess yourself on each. Each one is important for you to understand and eventually to master, if you are to move forward in your life.

Exercise 1 invites you to consider your confidence in your ability to set goals. Setting goals is the first step in change, because it requires you to envision a preferred condition. In order to set goals, you must have confidence that you can actually have a better life.

TASK: Rate your confidence in your ability to create a better life on a scale from 1 (completely confident) to 10 (no confidence). Then write down the reason you gave yourself that rating. Do you notice that your confidence in your ability to set goals has been diminishing? Can you identify the cause of the decline?

EXERCISE 2B – SELF-EFFICACY, ERODING

Exercise 2 invites you to consider your level of confidence in your ability to create effective plans. Goals are of no value until you can create the pathway to accomplish them. You might want to get to the top of the mountain, but until you can see your path up it, it will seem impossible to reach the top. You may have had big goals for yourself at some point in your life but your confidence in your ability to achieve them has been diminishing. You are losing confidence in your ability to make good things happen for yourself.

TASK: Rate your ability to make effective plans from 1 (completely confident) to 10 (no confidence). Then write down the reason you gave yourself that rating. If you see your confidence in your ability to plan diminishing, can you identify the cause?

EXERCISE 3B – SELF-EFFICACY, ERODING

Exercise 3 invites you to consider your level of confidence in your ability to make the right choices. You may have proven to yourself that you can set useful goals for yourself and even create quality plans. But, for some reason you are losing confidence in your ability to follow through. You may have made decisions that actually undermined your well-being. Or, you may have run into difficulties that were too difficult for you to resolve. For whatever reason, your confidence in your ability to stick with your plans has been eroding.

TASK: Rate your ability to make the right choices for yourself from 1 (completely confident) to 10 (no confidence). Then write down the reason you gave yourself that score. If you are seeing your confidence diminish in this area, can you identify the reason?

EXERCISE 4B – SELF-EFFICACY, ERODING

Exercise 4 invites you to consider your level of confidence in your ability to persevere. Even if you set goals, make effective plans, and make the right choices, it is only when you can hold that course and continue down that path that you will gain the reward of your effort in positive life change. You may have found yourself frequently distracted or simply lacking the ability to keep yourself engaged in the plan you know would be helpful for you to achieve. Perhaps you started many great diet plans but never completed any. Or, you sent out a bunch of résumés but never followed through on the interviews. In the process, you have damaged your confidence in your ability to effectively follow through. Your lack of confidence now interferes with your ability to start anything new.

TASK: Rate your confidence in your ability to follow through from 1 (completely confident) to 10 (no confidence). Then write down the reasons you gave yourself that score.

SESSION 3
EXERCISE 1C – SELF-EFFICACY, ERODING

Session 3 invites you to begin to shift from losing confidence in your ability to shape your life in a positive way to restoring confidence. Belief is the foundation of all successful action. You simply must believe. Let's get started.

Exercise 1 invites you to cultivate belief that life is your friend, that it holds many positive possibilities for your life. This may be challenging since your past might tell a different story. But, perhaps some of your past negative experiences were due to the fact that you were losing your belief that life was your ally. In order to regain confidence in your partnership with life, we invite you to take notice of all that life has provided for you and all of the ways it has supported you, rather than focusing on what didn't work out well.

TASK: Please make a list of all that life has provided for you in order to have a successful and powerful life. Be thoughtful. Consider the country in which you were born, the gifts and skills with which you were endowed, and all of the good things that have happened to you. Add to this list every day and open yourself to a stronger belief in your ability to partner with life in a positive manner.

EXERCISE 2C – SELF-EFFICACY, ERODING

Exercise 2 invites you to shift from having declining confidence in your ability to create a meaningful life to restoring confidence in yourself. It is likely that you have a clear understanding of the mistakes you have made and the choices that didn't work out. You may have a litany of dreams that didn't come true and of circumstances that have made life harder for you. But, you may not be seeing clearly how you have actively shaped your life for good. You may have overlooked times when you created success and when you used your gifts and abilities to make good things happen. It is critical that you are able to see your ability to make your life better. Your confidence rests on that foundation.

TASK: Make a list of all of the successes you have created for yourself. Be thoughtful and take your time. None is too small to add to the list. Don't even consider your failures and problems. Notice that you have been effective more often than you have noticed. You need to begin to see yourself as someone who has the ability to shape life in your best interest.

EXERCISE 3C – SELF-EFFICACY, ERODING

Exercise 3 invites you to shift from having diminishing confidence in your ability to effectively work with others to make positive things happen to believing in your skill to interact with the people in your life effectively and positively. While you might not always see it, you have had a positive impact on many people in your life and many people have had a positive influence on yours. You have formed alliances with people in the past that have worked out well for everyone and that have shaped their life and yours in a positive way. You may have partnered with someone to raise a family and can see how your children have been blessed by your commitment to them. You may have friends you reached out and supported when they were going through a hard time and who are on solid footing because of you. You may have had friends who encouraged you to believe in yourself and because of whom you achieved something important to you. Every one of those partnerships proves that you can make a difference in the lives of others and can invite others to make a difference in your own.

TASK: Make a list of all of those relationships that have worked out well. Noticing the positive impact you can have can begin to restore your confidence in yourself.

EXERCISE 4C – SELF-EFFICACY, ERODING

Exercise 4 invites you to shift from having weakening confidence in your ability to manage your circumstances to believing in your skill to make things better regardless of what life throws at you. It would be wonderful if life only provided you with abundant opportunities that required little effort or resourcefulness on your part. But rarely, if ever, does that occur. It is crucial that you believe that you can control your circumstances even when things are hard and your options are limited. In his classic book *Man's Search for Meaning*, Viktor Frankl pointed out that one of the fundamental building blocks of survival and thriving is to work with whatever control is available to you regardless of the circumstances. It is learning to see past the obstacles in order to see the opportunities and to leverage those to make things better. It is likely that you have done exactly that more often than you have noticed. You have found yourself in hard times and found a way to get through.

TASK: Make a list of some of the difficulties you have overcome in your life. Now, write down what opportunities you discovered in each one that allowed you to get through it. Seeing your resourcefulness is encouragement to believe you possess this skill and can continue to improve it.

SESSION 4
EXERCISE 1D – SELF-EFFICACY, ERODING

Session 4 will provide you with some basic, but important, skills to build on your foundation of confidence that you can, in fact, shape your world for the better.

Exercise 1 asks you to begin cultivating the skill of vision. Vision is built on the idea that you must envision what you want before you can make it happen. You aren't likely to lose weight until you can envision yourself thinner. You aren't likely to make much more money until you can envision your life with more money. Visioning requires increasing your confidence in yourself. You need to believe that your dreams can come true. If you don't believe, you won't dream or you will dream small.

TASK: Practice writing down a few things you want to make your life better. It doesn't matter at this point if they are ambitious or not. It is only important that you want them. Review your list every day this week and ask yourself if you believe you can actually make these things happen. Cross out those in which you don't believe. Refine your list to the two or three most important things you want to create for your life.

EXERCISE 2D – SELF-EFFICACY, ERODING

Exercise 2 invites you to begin cultivating confidence in your ability to thoughtfully and meaningfully plan. Change doesn't happen simply because you want something that you don't have. It doesn't have a chance of happening until you plan the pathway to make it happen. Plans break down a vision into small enough steps to be practical. Those steps must take into account your resources, skills, determination, obstacles, and perseverance. A plan that is too ambitious can set you up for certain failure. A plan that takes too long can be discouraging. A plan that requires resources that aren't available to you isn't practical. In order for you to gain confidence in your ability to successfully craft your life, you must have growing confidence in your ability to effectively plan.

TASK: Take one of the visions you listed in Exercise 1. Create a plan. Notice where you are having difficulties or setting yourself up for problems. Keep working on it until you can sit back, review it, and believe that you have what it takes to actually execute on it.

EXERCISE 3D – SELF-EFFICACY, ERODING

Exercise 3 invites you to begin cultivating confidence that you can actually follow through on your plans to the very end. If the journey toward your goals is abandoned, it fails to achieve the outcome you desired and becomes a discouragement for every future effort. On the other hand, completing what you have started and reaping the benefit of your effort is encouragement to take on another goal. Every time you set a vision, create a plan, and successfully execute it, your confidence in your ability to constructively shape your life will grow stronger. Hence, it is very important to start small and to create a series of successes. Working on your plan will require a lot of you. You will need to stay focused, learn to delay gratification, discipline yourself, and follow through to the very end. These are not skills that everyone has fully developed. Starting small will allow you to practice and master each one.

TASK: Take out your plan from the last session and begin putting it into practice. Notice what comes easy to you. Notice what does not. Keep focused on the outcome at the end of the plan and use it to encourage yourself to keep going. Make sure you succeed, because the outcome will be the natural expansion of your confidence.

EXERCISE 4D – SELF-EFFICACY, ERODING

Exercise 4 invites you to expand your self-confidence by celebrating, resting, reviewing, renewing, and expanding. When you achieve a goal that you set for yourself, be it big or small, it is reason to celebrate. Celebrations don't need to be wild and expensive. They can be as small as taking 30 minutes to appreciate yourself for the work you have done on your life. Celebrations help to break up the tasks of life into more bite-sized chunks. Next, rest.

TASK: Take a few days off. Don't take on your next vision until you have rested and renewed yourself. Use your rest time to review all that you learned on your journey. Write down what you learned about yourself, especially those things that you value and appreciate. Noticing your strengths and new skills will expand your resources for the next vision you take on and your confidence in yourself will grow. Now, when you are ready, take on your next project to make your life even better.

FACTOR – SELF-EFFICACY

This factor refers to your confidence in your ability to exert control over your own motivation, behavior, and social environment. People who have high self-efficacy see themselves as capable of shaping their world to suit themselves. Those who have low self-efficacy feel at the effect of the world around them.

SELF-ASSESSED RATING – TREADING WATER

You have confidence in our ability to manage yourself and your life as it currently exists, but not to make it better.

SESSION 1
EXERCISE 1A – SELF-EFFICACY, TREADING WATER

You are treading water in your life, partly because you lack sufficient confidence in your ability to exert control over your own motivation, behavior, and social environment to make further progress. You believe in your abilities enough to keep your life from falling into disarray, but you don't possess sufficient belief in yourself to make your life much better. In Session 1 we invite you to better understand why and how you ended up stuck. Let's get started.

Exercise 1 invites you to focus on your motivation to change and grow. It is likely that you find yourself lacking the motivation to make significant changes in your circumstances. You lack confidence that you can make your life much better than it is right now, and your lack of confidence in yourself undermines your ability to make constructive change. Perhaps you have wrestled with some thoughts about changes you might like to make, but haven't been able to muster sufficient desire to take on those projects. Now you doubt your ability to marshal your resources to move forward.

TASK: Make a list of goals and projects that you have had insufficient motivation to take on or complete.

EXERCISE 2A – SELF-EFFICACY, TREADING WATER

Exercise 2 invites you to focus on your behavior; notice the choices you are making and what your behavior says about your confidence in your ability to manage your world. It is likely that you have confidence in your ability to avoid making bad choices that would get you into trouble. You manage your finances reasonably well and have built stable, rewarding relationships. But, you may lack confidence in your ability to make choices that advance your life. You may notice that you haven't changed very much in quite some time. You haven't taken on much that would transform your life or take you to a new level of functioning. These unused skills may have eroded your confidence in your ability to make big changes.

TASK: List life choices you have made over the past ten years. Categorize them in terms of major changes, moderate changes, and slight changes. Do you see a pattern of avoiding taking on big changes?

EXERCISE 3A – SELF-EFFICACY, TREADING WATER

Exercise 3 invites you to consider the people with whom you have chosen to relate and their impact on your confidence in your ability to control your life. You may have surrounded yourself with people who are always pushing you to be and do more or those who are reasonably content with you and your relationship with them. The first group will continue to drive you to change and will challenge you to keep believing in your ability to grow. The second group will affirm what you have already done and invite you to be content. They may even suggest that you shouldn't invest in change lest you undermine the good things you have created for yourself. Such subtle messages can, over time, undermine your confidence in your ability to continue to shape your life.

TASK: Make a list of the top ten people with whom you relate; your best and closest friends. Now, write next to each either a C for those who challenge you to be more or an S for those who invite you to settle for things as they are. You might be surprised to see who shows up on each.

EXERCISE 4A – SELF-EFFICACY, TREADING WATER

Exercise 4 invites you to consider the circumstances of your life. There are two motivators of change: distress and vision. We are all more willing to change when things get bad enough. We are also willing to change when there is something we want so much that we must change to achieve it. Between the two is the "dead zone," where life is good enough such that much change is not necessary. This is one of the primary reasons people stop improving their lives. Living in the dead zone undermines their desire and confidence to move forward. You may find that while you recognize the value of making changes, you simply lack confidence in your desire to change your situation.

TASK: Put your current circumstances into one of three categories: distress (things are bad and must change), vision (things you want and can't have without change), dead zone (things are good enough as they are). If you find much of your life is in the dead zone, you know you lack confidence in your willingness to change.

SESSION 2

EXERCISE 1B – SELF-EFFICACY, TREADING WATER

The key to forward momentum in your life is your degree of confidence in your ability to make your life better. Without greater confidence, you simply won't move forward. Session 2 focuses your attention on different aspects of self-confidence and asks you to assess yourself on each. Each one is important for you to understand and to master if you are to begin to grow again.

Exercise 1 invites you to consider your confidence in your ability to set goals. Setting forward-looking goals is different than setting goals that prevent your life from declining. You may be very skilled at knowing what you don't want to happen in your life, but have far less confidence in your ability to set forward-looking ones. Many people have difficulty clarifying their dreams and desires. Their goals and ambitions are vague and ill-defined.

TASK: Rate your confidence in your ability to set clear and measurable goals for yourself on a scale from 1 (completely confident) to 10 (no confidence). Then write down the reason you gave yourself that rating. What makes it hard for you to set clear goals for your life?

EXERCISE 2B – SELF-EFFICACY, TREADING WATER

Exercise 2 invites you to consider your level of confidence in your ability to create plans that advance your life goals. You may be effective at planning the events necessary to maintain your life and to keep it from slipping into disarray. It is likely that you manage your time reasonably well and make sure you complete all that is necessary to sustain your current level of success and thriving. But, you may not have much faith in your ability to create adequate plans for advancing toward future goals. Proper planning is difficult when your goals are not clear. If you were planning a road trip and knew only that you wanted to go west, it would be very difficult to create an adequate plan. If you know the goal is San Francisco and you want to be there in ten days, you are much better prepared to create an effective plan. Moreover, if you aren't particularly motivated to achieve your goal because you are satisfied with your current situation, it is not likely you will put a lot of energy or effort into planning. The result is a lack of faith in yourself that you can properly plan for future changes.

TASK: Rate your ability to make effective plans from 1 (completely confident) to 10 (no confidence). Then write down what undermines your confidence in your ability to make effective plans for your future.

EXERCISE 3B – SELF-EFFICACY, TREADING WATER

Exercise 3 invites you to consider your level of confidence in your ability to make the right choices. You know you can make the right choices in many areas of your life because you are doing pretty well and your life is in relatively good shape. But, that does not necessarily mean that you have confidence in your ability to make the right choices for your future. If you knew you had ten units of potential for your life, how many are you currently using? Write down your answer. If you are treading water, the answer should be somewhere between five and seven. You know you have significantly more potential than your choices are extracting. For some reason, you have learned to coast instead of pedaling as hard as necessary to fulfill much of your ability and to make your life all that it could be. Your choices may reflect a level of acceptance for what is, rather than a commitment to achieve more.

TASK: Rate your ability to make the best choices for yourself from 1 (complete confidence) to 10 (no confidence). Reflect on your answer. Why did you give yourself that score?

EXERCISE 4B – SELF-EFFICACY, TREADING WATER

Exercise 4 invites you to consider your level of confidence in your ability to persevere. You have certainly demonstrated the ability to stick with many of your goals and plans. Without that skill, you would not have been as successful as you have been. However, that does not necessarily mean that you have demonstrated to yourself the ability to persevere in the pursuit of your own growth and development, especially if it is difficult, challenging, or putting at risk the comfort and success you have already attained. Often, growth requires risk and effort. You may have the ability to go to school and attain an advanced degree. But, it might require borrowing money and spending evenings and weekends in a classroom or doing homework. While you might have obtained the information about the program and even applied, you didn't follow through on securing the money. You didn't follow through because you don't really need the degree. But, as a result, you have limited your ability to advance in your career.

TASK: Rate your confidence in your ability to follow through from 1 (completely confident) to 10 (no confidence). Then write down the reasons you gave yourself that score.

SESSION 3

EXERCISE 1C – SELF-EFFICACY, TREADING WATER

Session 3 invites you to expand your confidence in your ability to shape your life beyond your current level of satisfaction, such that you cultivate more of your unused potential. Belief is the key to expanding your confidence. You must believe in yourself more than you do currently. Let's get started.

Exercise 1 invites you to cultivate belief that the future is your friend and that it holds much greater success than you have yet experienced. This might be difficult, because you have grown accustomed to and content with your current level of comfort. Perhaps you compare your life to others and see that you done well and have it pretty good. But, you aren't comparing your current situation to your potential and what you could be, do, and have. Life has provided you with ample opportunities, but these may be only a small percentage of what remains undiscovered. Your partnership with life needs to expand such that you begin to see the future as holding much more for you than you currently have. Only when you have greater belief in the goodness of life toward you, will you be willing to do what is necessary to go and get it.

TASK: Make a list of the top five ways life has been good and generous to you. Now, imagine that you multiply them times five. What might life hold in store for you? Let this idea excite you and fill you up with new possibilities and confidence.

EXERCISE 2C – SELF-EFFICACY, TREADING WATER

Exercise 2 invites you to increase your confidence in yourself to substantially expand your life beyond its current level of success and achievement. It is likely that you are proud of yourself for all that you have accomplished, and you should be. You have done well with your life. But, you may have overlooked one of the most important lessons to have learned from your success: That you created it. You did not get where you are without taking on challenges, putting out significant effort, and taking big risks. You weren't lucky. You set goals, made plans, and worked hard. You pushed yourself when things were tough and hung in there when you hit roadblocks. The big lesson to extract from your journey was your tremendous ability to actively shape your life into what it is today. Seeing that clearly should feed your confidence that you can keep using those skills to continue to expand your success and happiness.

TASK: Make a list of the ten greatest achievements of your lifetime. Next to each, write down some of the lessons you learned from doing so.

EXERCISE 3C – SELF-EFFICACY, TREADING WATER

Exercise 3 invites to you increase your confidence in your ability to work effectively with others to expand your world beyond your current level of comfort. You have a history of attracting people into your life and relating to them in a way that has allowed you to reach your current level of comfort and success. It is likely that you have left some people behind on your journey because they either undermined your progress or couldn't (or wouldn't) keep up with you. You have also turned to people for advice and assistance when you had a goal you wanted to achieve. Your history of relating to people in a way that allowed them to assist you in your growth, and assisted them in their growth, should bolster your confidence that you can forge new alliances and better use your current relationships to move your life from treading water to growing.

TASK: Make a list of the five most valuable relationships you have in helping you to expand your life. Write down next to each how you found and built that relationship.

EXERCISE 4C – SELF-EFFICACY, TREADING WATER

Exercise 4 invites you to expand your confidence in your ability to deal with adversity and difficulty powerfully and successfully. Advancing your life is often difficult, demanding, and not without adversity. It is often the anticipation of those obstacles and the difficulty we envision in overcoming them that undermines our confidence in moving forward. This can be especially true when you have achieved a fair amount of security and success. Facing difficulty requires creativity, ingenuity, and resourcefulness; skills that are not often cultivated in less challenging circumstances. Seeing that not only have you already overcome adversity in the past, but may have learned some of your most useful and valuable lessons from doing so, will enhance your confidence that it is worth facing (and overcoming) any adversity you might encounter as you reengage the journey to improve your life.

TASK: Make a list of some of the adversity you faced and overcame in the past, and some of the lessons you learned from having done so.

SESSION 4
EXERCISE 1D – SELF-EFFICACY, TREADING WATER

Session 4 will provide you with some skills that will help you enhance your confidence in moving from treading water to growing in your life.

Exercise 1 will ask you strengthen your ability to envision your preferred future. It is unlikely that your life will be much better or bigger than your vision for it. Too often, the thing that limits the quality of your life is that you haven't dared to create a big enough vision for it. Instead, you have settled for less than you could have. We encourage you to dream a bigger dream for your life. Make a list of all you have accomplished that is important to you. Now, ask yourself what more you might want to achieve. Don't be practical. Don't assess the cost. Simply live with the question: What do I want that I don't have?

TASK: Write down whatever comes to mind. See if you come up with some new vision for your life that would motivate you to get out of the dead zone and start moving forward again. If you don't come up with much, ask your friends and family for ideas.

EXERCISE 2D – SELF-EFFICACY, TREADING WATER

Exercise 2 invites you to expand your confidence in your ability to creatively and effectively plan for the changes you intend to make. Maintaining your current level of success and comfort doesn't require making many plans, at least not the kind you need to make if you are ready for meaningful change. You may have grown accustomed to planning how to maintain what you have. But in the past, you created robust and meaningful plans in order to achieve your ambitious goals. Perhaps you can recall one or two of the plans you used in the past. You may have set out to create your career and so had a plan that required securing an entry level job, learning new skills, asking for more opportunity, and rising through the ranks to get where you are now.

TASK: Recalling some of those plans can be helpful in fortifying your confidence that you can do the same thing now with your new dreams.

EXERCISE 3D – SELF-EFFICACY, TREADING WATER

Exercise 3 invites you to expand your confidence in your ability to get into action and to actively improve the quality and meaning of your life. You may have been "resting" for quite some time. "Resting" is a much better way of thinking about your life than being "stuck." Stuck would imply you have external obstacles that are limiting your progress. Resting suggests you have been marshaling your resources, fortifying your courage, and preparing. If you look back at your life, you will discover that there were other times when you rested before moving forward.

TASK: Make a list of some of those times in order to expand your confidence that those resting times were followed by progress. If you left your comfort to reach for more in the past, you can do so again.

EXERCISE 4D – SELF-EFFICACY, TREADING WATER

Exercise 4 invites you to expand your confidence in your ability to celebrate yourself. It can be easy to forget the grandeur of your visions, the thoughtfulness you have demonstrated, the effort you have expended, the obstacles you have overcome, and the victories you have achieved. You created your life with your own effort and resourcefulness. You worked through difficult problems and disciplined yourself to do things that were not pleasant. Celebrating yourself can help you remember the beauty of your life and how precious it is. Celebrating yourself can remind you not to settle for good when you can have better. Celebrating can inspire you to take the next hill.

TASK: Make a list of ten accomplishments you have had over your lifetime of which you are proud.

FACTOR – SELF-EFFICACY

This factor refers to your confidence in your ability to exert control over your own motivation, behavior, and social environment. People who have high self-efficacy see themselves as capable of shaping their world to suit themselves. Those who have low self-efficacy feel at the effect of the world around them.

SELF-ASSESSED RATING – GROWING

You have confidence that you can not only manage yourself and your life, but can also expand it. However, you have one or two issues over which you lack confidence.

SESSION 1

EXERCISE 1A – SELF-EFFICACY, GROWING

You are growing in your life. Things are good and getting better. You have a great deal of which to be proud. However, you aren't yet thriving. As least part of the reason you are not thriving is because you lack some confidence in your ability to get there. Session 1 will assist you in exploring some of the reasons that may undermine your full confidence. Let's get started.

Exercise 1 invites you to focus on your motivation to thrive. Let's face it; your life is pretty good. In fact, it might be better than it has ever been. You may be making more money than you ever expected to make. You might have wonderfully satisfying relationships. You might be in a career that is interesting and expanding. In such pleasant circumstances, it is easy to lose confidence in your motivation to stretch for more.

TASK: Assess your motivation to thrive. Be honest with yourself. Do you have the desire for more?

EXERCISE 2A – SELF-EFFICACY, GROWING

Exercise 2 invites you to assess your behavior; notice the choices you are making and what they say about your confidence in your ability to thrive. Our actions speak louder than our words. You may be telling yourself that you are motivated to thrive, but an honest assessment of your behavior might prove otherwise. Can you see choices you are making that are good but not the very best? Can you see challenges you are not taking on that would make your life even more wonderful? Can you see any issues you have been unwilling to resolve because they don't seem worth the effort?

TASK: Make a list of all of the choices you see yourself making that indicate you lack confidence in yourself to take on thriving.

EXERCISE 3A – SELF-EFFICACY, GROWING

Exercise 3 invites you to consider the people in your life and their impact on your confidence to thrive. The important people in your life exert a powerful influence on your confidence. They have the ability to push you to take on more or to entice you to settle for less than the very best. Sometimes friends and family may attempt to hold you back, because they fear the changes you will make as you move toward thriving will negatively impact your relationship with them. They are showing greater concern for themselves than for you. Assess your relationship with the people in your life.

TASK: Make a list of the people whom you can count on to push you to be your very best. Make another list of people who might be holding you back. These are anchors you may need to jettison because they undermine your confidence.

EXERCISE 4A – SELF-EFFICACY, GROWING

Exercise 4 invites you to consider the circumstances of your life. You have done well. Your life is growing. You don't have any obvious distress that would motivate change. Your pleasant circumstances can undermine your confidence in your ability to change, because you might fear messing up or sacrificing what you have to get what you want. Thriving might require letting go of some things that you enjoy. It might require taking on new challenges. It might require leaving some people behind. If you are honest with yourself, you might discover you have a few things that you aren't willing to deal with or surrender in order to thrive.

TASK: Do an honest assessment. Write down anything that comes to mind.

SESSION 2

EXERCISE 1B – SELF-EFFICACY, GROWING

The key to pressing forward toward thriving is expanding your confidence in your ability to make your life all that it can be. Without greater confidence, you are likely to remain content as you are. In Session 2 we focus your attention on different aspects of self-confidence and ask you to assess yourself on each. Each one is important for you to understand and to master if you are to press on toward thriving.

Exercise 1 invites you to consider your confidence in setting goals. Obviously, you have been good at setting goals for yourself. Otherwise, you would not be doing as well as you are. However, there may be one or two areas where you are avoiding setting goals worthy of your life. You may be fearful of addressing these issues because you suspect they might be especially difficult to resolve. You may be with a partner who is holding you back in some way. You don't want to address the issue because you have a deep sense of loyalty and love for them and you don't want to disrupt things. Or, you might be loyal to your boss and so have been unwilling to move to the next phase of your career that would require going to another company or starting your own business. Only you know where you have lacked the confidence to set the bigger goal for yourself.

TASK: Rate your level of confidence in your ability to set clear goals that will move you toward thriving from 1 (completely confident) to 10 (no confidence). Then write down the reason you gave yourself that rating.

EXERCISE 2B – SELF-EFFICACY, GROWING

Exercise 2 invites you to assess your ability to actually create the plans needed to move you toward thriving. You may have a clear view of how your life would be if you were fully thriving, but, for some reason, have not captured the pathway to get there in a concrete plan. Perhaps you have been avoiding creating a plan because you know it would take you one step closer to making an important decision. Or, perhaps you don't have confidence in making those plans because you would be entering areas where you lack experience and expertise. Regardless, without a clear plan, it is not likely that you will move much farther along in your journey.

TASK: Rate your ability to make an effective plan that will take you from growing to thriving from 1 (completely confident) to 10 (no confidence). Then write down why you have not created an effective plan.

EXERCISE 3B – SELF-EFFICACY, GROWING

Exercise 3 invites you to consider your confidence in your ability to make the right choices when the stakes are high. You haven't risen to your level of success without proving that you can make difficult choices, but sometimes we find ourselves in circumstances where the decisions we must make are daunting. In order to attain your dream job, you will need to relocate your family to a different part of the country. Or, to exercise your unique ability to see financial opportunity, you will need to cash out a large portion of your life savings. You are torn between enjoying the path you are on and taking that one big risk that could make things even better or end in disaster.

TASK: Rate your level of confidence in your ability to make those hard decisions from 1 (completely confident) to 10 (no confidence). What issue or issues are you struggling with right now?

EXERCISE 4B – SELF-EFFICACY, GROWING

Exercise 4 invites you to consider your level of confidence in your ability to persevere. You have proven many times that you can take on difficult life challenges and see them through to the end. But, you may have one or two challenges that require an unusual amount of dedication or persistence and from which you have backed away. Perhaps you know that you should go back to school to get that advanced degree, but the thought of giving up all of those evenings and weekends to school work discourages you from signing up. You just aren't confident that you have what it takes to stick with a project that will take years to complete. You are concerned that you will start it and then give up halfway through and all of your effort will be for nothing.

TASK: Rate your confidence in your ability to persevere from 1 (completely confident) to 10 (no confidence).

SESSION 3
EXERCISE 1C – SELF-EFFICACY, GROWING

Session 3 invites you to sufficiently expand your confidence in your ability to shape your life such that you are ready to take on whatever challenge is required for you to fully thrive. You must believe in your potential so much that you will not settle for anything less than your very best life. Let's get started.

Exercise 1 invites you to cultivate your belief that life is your friend and so offers you even more than you currently have. Your success in life has been abundant. You have witnessed many times how life has provided you with opportunity to change and to grow, and that taking advantage of those opportunities is the reason you have such an abundant life. Shouldn't you extrapolate from those experiences that life has even greater abundance available to you? Let yourself be filled up with a sense of wonder about the goodness of your life now.

TASK: Write down the five things for which you are most grateful. Now, imagine there is still more. What would the "more" be? Write it down.

EXERCISE 2C – SELF-EFFICACY, GROWING

Exercise 2 invites you to expand your confidence in yourself to move your life beyond growing and into thriving. You have done such a wonderful job with your life. You have taken on opportunities. You have overcome obstacles. You have stuck with your plans. You have been resourceful. Why should you stop now? Haven't you proven to yourself that you are capable of making steady and significant progress?

TASK: Make a list of ten ways that you have improved your life. Next, write down some of the skills and qualities you used to make those improvements. Can you see how equipped you are to take on whatever is next on your journey?

EXERCISE 3C – SELF-EFFICACY, GROWING

Exercise 3 invites you to expand your confidence in your ability to forge relationships that challenge you to take on new and important growth opportunities. You have a history of inviting people into your life who have been wonderful resources for you on your life journey. They have believed in you. They have encouraged you to believe in yourself. They have given assistance, made introductions, and shared their resources with you. Some of them saw possibilities in you that you didn't see in yourself, and it was the push they gave you that got you over whatever obstacles were in your way. It is useful to review and appreciate those friends and family, and to see the value of having people in your life who push you to reach for more.

TASK: Make a list of at least five people who have pushed you to do the things that have made you successful. Review that list and notice how you found those people and how you invited them into your life. Notice how you engaged with them and what you asked of them. You have proven the ability to attract powerful people who will push you forward.

EXERCISE 4C – SELF-EFFICACY, GROWING

Exercise 4 invites you to expand your confidence in your ability to deal with obstacles and adversity in a powerful and effective manner. It is likely that the reason you are growing but not thriving is because you are facing one obstacle that you have not yet dealt with. This one might seem especially daunting and to be much riskier than others with which you have dealt. But, you may have forgotten how resourceful and courageous you have been in overcoming obstacles in the past and how many times those obstacles seemed at the time to be especially large and dangerous.

TASK: Make a list of five obstacles you overcame. Try to put yourself back in the place when you were facing each one. Remember how frightened you were and how difficult it was to take it on. Then recall the feeling of mastery when you moved into and through it. You have many reasons to be confident in your ability to take on any issue life throws at you.

SESSION 4
EXERCISE 1D – SELF-EFFICACY, GROWING

Session 4 will provide you with the skills needed to enhance your confidence to move from growing to thriving in your life.

Exercise 1 will ask you to strengthen your ability to envision your life as fully thriving. Your life is good as it is, but you know there is more. One of the ways you may be avoiding thriving is to avoid imagining it. When you can clearly see how wonderful your life will be, you will have greater confidence to move forward.

TASK: Write down what your life will be like when you are fully thriving. Notice any reluctance to include something because it might seem to be too big, too much, or too hard to obtain. Include it anyway. Practice envisioning your thriving life until it feels real.

EXERCISE 2D – SELF-EFFICACY, GROWING

Exercise 2 invites you to expand your confidence in your ability to create effective plans for the changes you need to make to fully thrive. You have made plans for many of the challenges you have successfully taken on in your life. Those plans were your roadmap to get where you are. You know how to properly evaluate your resources and to create a plan that takes into account your tolerance for risk while moving you forward. It is your history of making effective plans that should expand your confidence in building an effective plan for the challenge standing in your way of thriving.

TASK: Review some of the plans you have used in the past. Now, apply those same principles to the issue you need to address. How would you solve this problem? How would you get to where you know you need to go? What would you do first? Next?

EXERCISE 3D – SELF-EFFICACY, GROWING

Exercise 3 invites you to expand your confidence in your ability to get into action on whatever issue needs to be addressed in order for you to move toward thriving. You know how to make progress in improving the quality of your life. You have done quite well taking on one issue after another, and with positive results. Yet, on one or two issues, you seem to lack the confidence to get moving. Perhaps you are worried about the potential downside of the change you know you need to make. Or, you are heading into new and unfamiliar territory and find yourself being overly cautious in taking action. The best way to expand your confidence is to review times in your past when you put your growth plan into action and experienced the benefit of the change you sought. This has been the key to your growth and the reason your life is going so well.

TASK: Make a list of five times when you got into action and produced a wonderful result for yourself. Use those successes to bolster your confidence.

EXERCISE 4D – SELF-EFFICACY, GROWING

Exercise 4 invites you to expand your confidence in your ability to break through upper limits. Everyone gets used to a certain amount of success, happiness, love, and peace. When life offers us more, we can sabotage ourselves in order to stay in our comfort zone. You may need to learn to expand your capacity to experience more before you can break through to thriving.

TASK: Notice how you feel about the idea of thriving. Do you find yourself feeling anxious as you consider your expanded success, happiness, etc.? If so, practice envisioning that success for 15 minutes each day for the next few weeks. As you see yourself thriving, breathe deeply and slowly. This allows your body to acclimate to the next level of success.

EXERCISE SERIES: ACHIEVEMENT-STRIVING

FACTOR – ACHIEVEMENT-STRIVING

This trait speaks to your ability to harness your energy and skills in a manner that can produce positive results. Those who have developed this skill are able to maximize their productivity. They use their time and resources judiciously and minimize wasted time and effort. Those who are low in this skill find themselves wishing for things to occur, procrastinating, and wasting time. They have difficulty getting their act together sufficiently to make things happen.

SELF-ASSESSED RATING – HANGING ON

You have no ability to harness your energy and gifts so as to successfully achieve the goals you must master.

SESSION 1

EXERCISE 1A – ACHIEVEMENT-STRIVING, HANGING ON

You are hanging on by your fingernails primarily because you have been unsuccessful at harnessing your energy and skills so as to produce positive results in your life. You may be largely unaware of your skills and useful energy and/or have been failing to utilize them in a constructive manner. Session 1 will ask you to assess aspects of your energy so they become clearer to you. Let's get started.

Exercise 1 invites you to assess your physical energy. People with high physical energy are always in action. They stay busy, don't waste much time, and are always on the go. Those with low physical energy are slow moving and largely inactive.

TASK: Make a list of where would you put yourself on this continuum? Possessing high physical energy is very helpful in shaping your life.

EXERCISE 2A – ACHIEVEMENT-STRIVING, HANGING ON

Exercise 2 invites you to assess your level of mental energy. People with high mental energy are full of ideas. Their mind is active in thinking about the future, creatively solving problems, and scanning for opportunity. People with low mental energy tend to like repetition and predictability. They resist change and have few, if any, thoughts about the future. They tend to be rigid in their thinking and resistant to new ideas.

TASK: How would you assess your mental energy? High mental energy is necessary if you are to move beyond hanging on by your fingernails to a more full and complete way of living.

EXERCISE 3A – ACHIEVEMENT-STRIVING, HANGING ON

Exercise 3 invites you to consider the quality of your energy. Whether you know it or not, you are always exuding either positive or negative energy. Positive energy motivates, excites, energizes, and attracts others. It is the power that moves things forward. Negative energy shows up as complaining, feeling defeated, showing resentfulness, and resistance to change. Everyone vacillates between the two to some extent, but also has some level of either positive or negative energy that characterizes the general way you see your life and the world around you.

TASK: Rate the quality of your energy on a 5-point scale. One end is extreme negative energy and the other is extreme positive energy. You may have grown accustomed to the energy given off such that it doesn't seem as negative as it truly might be. It would be wise for you to ask five other people who you trust to be honest with you to rate your energy on the same scale. Negative energy will inhibit your ability to improve your life.

EXERCISE 4A – ACHIEVEMENT-STRIVING, HANGING ON

Exercise 4 invites you to consider the quality of your spiritual energy. We differentiate spiritual from religious. By spiritual energy, we mean your level of faith in something bigger than yourself, some higher purpose, or meaning in life. You may be a person who lacks any sense of purpose, calling, or faith, and so have little spiritual energy to call on. On the other hand, you might have a great deal of spiritual energy that is demonstrated by a belief that life is meant to be good and abundant, and that you have a responsibility to live up to the potential with which you have been entrusted.

TASK: Rate your level of spiritual energy on a 5-point scale. One end is the absence of faith and a sense of a higher purpose for your life. At the other end, is a deep belief that your life is meant to be abundant and that you have a strong sense of calling to invest your life wisely. This energy is critical to growth and development. Harnessing your spiritual energy can supply courage and tenacity when facing life's challenges.

SESSION 2
EXERCISE 1B – ACHIEVEMENT-STRIVING, HANGING ON

Session 2 focuses your attention on your skills and resources. It is very important to notice and properly assess the resources you have available. These are often overlooked and so aren't available to you when you need them. You may have tools in your toolbox of which you are unaware or you have forgotten how to use. Life frequently requires the use of all of them. Let's get started.

Exercise 1 invites you to focus on your education. Education is a remarkable gift for many reasons. First, education teaches us skills like focusing our attention, delaying gratification, working with others, and following directions. Second, your education has provided you with information and knowledge outside of what you might normally encounter in your daily life. In that manner, education has expanded your perspective on the world. Education also has equipped you with skills that you need to be useful and to provide for yourself. Sometimes people undervalue their education because they didn't stay in the process and achieve as much as others have. Comparing in this way isn't helpful. It is much better to be appreciative of the education you have and to consider the gifts you received from it.

TASK: Make a list of ten benefits from your education.

EXERCISE 2B – ACHIEVEMENT-STRIVING, HANGING ON

Exercise 2 invites you to focus on your experience. As with education, experience is a valuable teacher, whatever your experience has been. You have met new people, worked in different settings, taken on different challenges, and had some victories and some losses. There are always a multitude of extremely useful lessons, skills, and character development that flows from your experience. It would be unfortunate if you view most or all of your experience as negative or bad and so don't appreciate the value you have gained from it. Quite often, those life lessons prove to be of even greater value than your education because they are more applicable to real-life experiences. The more times you face a challenge, the better equipped you are to meet it the next time. You know what hasn't worked and are more likely to discover something new that will.

TASK: Look back over your life and make a list of fifteen experiences that come to mind. Then write next to each some valuable lesson you learned.

EXERCISE 3B – ACHIEVEMENT-STRIVING, HANGING ON

Exercise 3 invites you to focus on your self-care. While it is true that right now you are hanging on by your fingernails, that does not mean that you lack the skills to take care of yourself. Taking care of yourself is your most basic and fundamental responsibility. You can't do very much to make your life better unless you can take care of yourself. The better you take care of yourself, the more you have to offer to others and to the world around you. Since your life might currently be in disarray, you might fail to notice all of the ways you have cared for yourself in the past and care for yourself now. These can be as simple as making sure you have the food you need and that you get enough rest. They also include making the money you need and building a network of people who care for you.

TASK: Take the time to make a list of all of the ways you have and now care for yourself. Don't leave anything out. Seeing your ability to care for yourself is critical if you are going to extend that care to take on the challenges you need to address in your life.

EXERCISE 4B – ACHIEVEMENT-STRIVING, HANGING ON

Exercise 4 invites you to focus on your interpersonal skill. People are some of the most valuable resources we have in our lives. It is so easy for everyone to get caught in their own patterns of thinking about themselves and about life. We also fall into habits and patterns that limit change. Interacting with people forces us to think new thoughts, to soften some of our habits, and to adapt to new challenges. The people in your life can be your greatest cheerleaders, rooting for your success. They can encourage you and pick you up when you are discouraged. They can share their resources and assistance with you when you are in need. It is easy to take this resource for granted and so not use it to your best benefit.

TASK: Make a list of ten people you know who have been helpful to you in the past and/or are helpful to you now. Appreciate them as a resource that can help you move from hanging on by your fingernails to the next level of development, even if you don't yet know how to make them more useful.

SESSION 3

EXERCISE 1C – ACHIEVEMENT-STRIVING, HANGING ON

Session 3 introduces you to the concepts of harnessing your energy and resources. You are hanging on by your fingernails, not necessarily because you lack resources and skill but because you aren't harnessing them adequately. Let's get started.

Exercise 1 invites you to learn the skill of noticing your energy and resources. This was the point of Sessions 1 and 2, but now we want you to see that this must become a daily practice if you are to improve your life. Unless you learn to see that you have energy and resources, there is no way you can begin to deploy them in your life. It is highly likely that you hardly ever notice what you have because you are too focused on what you lack.

TASK: We invite you now to keep a daily record of times when you notice that you actually have energy and resources you could use to make your life better. Do this every day for the next week.

EXERCISE 2C – ACHIEVEMENT-STRIVING, HANGING ON

Exercise 2 invites you to properly value your energy and resources. You may have a bias to assume that, even if you have some limited energy and resources, they are of little value and their use would not make much of a positive difference in your life. Such a negative, disparaging view of your strengths makes it very difficult to harness their power. Sessions 1 and 2 should have opened your eyes to value your energy and resources more highly. But, that is only the beginning. You must learn to appreciate every manifestation of your energy and resources in order to see them as useful tools with which you can stop your decline and can build a satisfying and meaningful life.

TASK: Take out your list from Exercise 1 and read it through. Notice if you tend to downplay their value or to see them for the utility they provide. Write down next to each one some ways you could use them to make needed improvements in your life. We aren't asking you to change anything other than your ability to appreciate what you already possess.

EXERCISE 3C – ACHIEVEMENT-STRIVING, HANGING ON

Exercise 3 invites you to consider the value of sharpening your energy and your skills. Just as tools become less useful when they grow rusty and dull, your resources need constant attention if they are going to continue to be valuable and to grow in value. Regardless of how negative your energy might be, there are things you do that either feed the negativity or the movement toward more positive energy. Similarly, you may be neglecting to use your resources such that they fall into disrepair or you may be practicing with them in order to keep them sharp and vibrant. The choice is always yours. Make a list of things you do that influence your energy and note which make it more negative and which make it more positive.

TASK: Make a list of the things you do with your resources and note which sharpen them and which make them dull and less useful.

EXERCISE 4C – ACHIEVEMENT-STRIVING, HANGING ON

Exercise 4 invites you to consider the value of expanding your energy and resources. Whatever positive energy and resources you currently have are only the foundation for what you can add. You have been learning and growing since you were born. You have added to your skills and resources over and over again. There was a time when you didn't know how to smile. When you mastered smiling, people attended to you much more frequently. You couldn't roll over. Then you learned to crawl and then to walk and then to run. As your resources and skills expanded so did your world. But, you may have forgotten the connection between expanding your energy and resources and the expansion of your life. At some point you may have become content or lazy and stopped expanding your skills.

TASK: Review your life for the past 10 years. What skills have you added? What resources have you developed? What have you done to expand those skills that you have?

SESSION 4
EXERCISE 1D – ACHIEVEMENT-STRIVING, HANGING ON

Session 4 focuses your attention on ways you could deploy your energy and skills to create positive results in your life. We are introducing you to these ideas knowing that you might not be ready yet to use them. But, understanding the path ahead of you is helpful as you prepare to change and grow.

Exercise 1 invites you to learn the value of determined outcomes. While it is important to have skills and resources, they only become useful when you decide to do something that requires them. If you aren't interested in changing your life in any way, you aren't likely to deploy many of the resources you possess.

TASK: Assess your level of acceptance with life as it is now. Are you content with things as they are? We hope not, because your assessment indicates that without corrective action on your part, your situation is likely to get worse. The fact that you are taking this exercise suggests you have some desire to change. But, exactly what do you want to change?

EXERCISE 2D – ACHIEVEMENT-STRIVING, HANGING ON

Exercise 2 invites you to consider the skills required to make the change you might want to make. One of the reasons people fail when they set out to make a change is because they haven't considered the skills needed to make that change. If you set your sights on running a marathon, you should first assess your physical condition. If you have been sedentary for a long time, you won't have the skills to enter the race tomorrow. To try to do so would only set you up for disappointment and lead to discouragement about any change you might consider.

TASK: Practice this skill by making up a few changes you might be considering, and then listing some of the skills and resources you might need in order to be successful.

EXERCISE 3D – ACHIEVEMENT-STRIVING, HANGING ON

Exercise 3 invites you to consider the energy required to make the changes you might want to make. Having sufficient resources and skills isn't enough to be successful in making your life better. You have to actually do something. Getting in action requires energy. Or, more accurately, it requires positive energy. If you don't believe you can make the change you desire, it will be very difficult, if not impossible to get started and to continue to stay in action. Positive energy keeps saying "I can do this." That voice is like having your own cheerleader who encourages you to keep trying. Everyone has an inner voice that is saying something.

TASK: Ask yourself what does your inner voice say to you? Does it feed your positive energy or detract from it?

EXERCISE 4D – ACHIEVEMENT-STRIVING, HANGING ON

Exercise 4 invites you to consider the value of possessing a feedback loop. This is a simple but important concept. A feedback loop allows you to assess where you are succeeding, where you are not, and why. It allows you to learn lessons from your effort and to make course corrections. It tells you when your resources are adequate and when you need to add to them in order to be successful. A realistic feedback look allows you to keep your energy and resources engaged, and to modify and alter your decisions so as to increase the likelihood of your success. Many people lack an adequate feedback loop because they get stuck in either/or thinking. They have either succeeded or failed. They don't have the ability to stay in the game, and to make subtle but critical shifts in how they deploy their energy and resources depending on how circumstances change.

TASK: Assess the health of your feedback loop. How good are you at properly assessing your situation, seeing where you are winning and where you are not, and then adapting your resources and energy accordingly? If this is not a strong skill. it will be one you need to expand.

FACTOR – ACHIEVEMENT-STRIVING

This trait speaks to your ability to harness your energy and skills in a manner that can produce positive results. Those who have developed this skill are able to maximize their productivity. They use their time and resources judiciously and minimize wasted time and effort. Those who are low in this skill find themselves wishing for things to occur, procrastinating, and wasting time. They have difficulty getting their act together sufficiently to make things happen.

SELF-ASSESSED RATING – ERODING

You have progressively less ability to harness your energy and gifts so as to successfully achieve your goals.

SESSION 1
EXERCISE 1A – ACHIEVEMENT-STRIVING, ERODING

You are eroding largely because you are not sufficiently harnessing your energy and skills so as to reverse your downward slide toward a more stable and useful way of living. You may be only slightly aware of your skills and useful energy and/or have been only marginally successful in utilizing them in a constructive manner. It is more likely that you are able to see how those around you have been successful at this than to see these abilities in yourself. Session 1 will invite you to assess aspects of your energy and skills so they become clearer to you. Let's get started.

Exercise 1 invites you to assess your physical energy. People with high physical energy are always in action. They stay busy shaping their lives and seem always busy. Those with low physical energy are slow moving or inactive. They have a lot of time on their hands and tend to waste opportunity. It is likely that you see others with more physical energy than you currently possess. You might envy their productivity. Your ability to see their energy and to compare it to your own is helpful because you can learn from them how to notice and harness your physical energy.

TASK: List five friends or family members who seem to have more physical energy than do you. What do you imagine causes them to be more energetic than are you?

EXERCISE 2A – ACHIEVEMENT-STRIVING, ERODING

Exercise 2 invites you to assess your level of mental energy. People with high mental energy are full of thoughts and ideas. It is as if their mind is always thinking about what they want and how they will get it. They are actively engaged in solving problems and moving forward. Those with low mental energy don't seem to have many thoughts about their future, or how to make things happen. They can't be bothered with thinking about their problems and issues. Again, you might be able to see friends and family who have more mental energy than you have. If so, use this comparison to study the difference their active mental energy has in shaping their success in life.

TASK: List five friends or family members who seem to have more mental energy than do you. What causes them to be more energetic than you?

EXERCISE 3A – ACHIEVEMENT-STRIVING, ERODING

Exercise 3 invites you to consider the quality of your energy. Your energy can be highly negative, highly positive, or anywhere in between. Perhaps you know someone who has extreme negative energy. All they talk about is what is wrong with them, others, and the world. They are filled with complaints and see themselves as helpless to make things better. People with high positive energy believe their lives are good, and that they are capable of getting almost anything they want, if they are willing to try hard enough. They have a "can do" attitude. Consider the quality of your energy.

TASK: Rate it on a 5-point scale. One end is extremely negative. The other end is extremely positive. Where would you put yourself? List five friends or family members who have more positive energy than do you. Why is their energy more positive than is yours?

EXERCISE 4A – ACHIEVEMENT-STRIVING, ERODING

Exercise 4 invites you to consider the quality of your spiritual energy. Spiritual energy has nothing to do with being religious. By spiritual energy, we mean your level of faith in something bigger than yourself, or some higher purpose or meaning in life. You may be a person who lacks any sense of purpose, calling, or faith, and so have little spiritual energy to call on. On the other hand, you might have a great deal of spiritual energy that is demonstrated by a belief that life is meant to be good and abundant, and that you have a responsibility to live up to the potential with which you have been entrusted.

TASK: Rate your level of spiritual energy on a 5-point scale. One end is the absence of faith and a sense of a higher purpose for your life. At the other end is a deep belief that your life is meant to be abundant, and that you have a strong sense of calling to invest your life wisely. This energy is critical in growth and development. List five people you know who seem to have high spiritual energy. How does it contribute to their lives?

SESSION 2
EXERCISE 1B – ACHIEVEMENT-STRIVING, ERODING

Session 2 focuses your attention on your skills and resources. It is critical that you notice and properly assess the resources you have available. These are often overlooked and so aren't available to you when you need them. You may have tools in your toolbox of which you are unaware or have forgotten how to use. Life frequently requires the use of all of them. It is likely that you are better able to see the skills and resources of others than your own. Let's get started.

Exercise 1 invites you to focus on your education. Education is a remarkable gift for many reasons. First, education teaches us skills like focusing our attention, delaying gratification, working with others, and following directions. Second, your education has provided you with information and knowledge outside of what you might normally encounter in your day to day life. In that manner, education has expanded your perspective on the world. Education also has equipped you with skills that you need to be useful and to provide for yourself. You may undervalue your education because you compare it to that of others and feel inadequate. Comparing in this way isn't helpful, because instead of using what you have, you tend to diminish its value. It is much better to be appreciative of the education you have and to consider the gifts you received from it.

TASK: Make a list of ten benefits from your education.

EXERCISE 2B – ACHIEVEMENT-STRIVING, ERODING

Exercise 2 invites you to focus on your experience. As with education, experience is a valuable teacher whatever your experience has been. You have met new people, worked in different settings, taken on different challenges, and had some victories and some losses. There are always a multitude of extremely useful lessons, skills, and character development that flows from your experience. It would be unfortunate if you view most or all of your experience as negative or bad, and so don't appreciate the value you have gained from it. Quite often, those life lessons prove to be of even greater value than your education, because they are more applicable to real life experiences. The more times you face a challenge, the better equipped you are to meet it the next time. You know what hasn't worked and are more likely to discover something new that will. If you compare your experiences to others and feel less prepared, you are undermining your confidence in the value of your own experience.

TASK: Look back over your life and make a list of 15 experiences that come to mind. Then write, next to each, some valuable lesson you learned.

EXERCISE 3B – ACHIEVEMENT-STRIVING, ERODING

Exercise 3 invites you to focus on your self-care. The fact that you are eroding indicates that you aren't taking adequate care of yourself. Taking care of yourself is your most basic and fundamental responsibility. You can't do very much to make your life better until you can take care of yourself. The better you take care of yourself, the more you have to offer to others and to the world around you. When your life is eroding, it is likely that your ability to care for yourself has been overwhelmed by difficult circumstances. In such a situation it is easy to lose confidence in your ability. These can be as simple as making sure you have the food you need, and that you get enough rest. They also include making the money you need, and building a network of people who care for you.

TASK: Take the time to make a list of all of the ways you now care for yourself. Don't leave anything out. Seeing your ability to care for yourself is critical if you are going to extend that care to take on the challenges you need to address in your life.

EXERCISE 4B – ACHIEVEMENT-STRIVING, ERODING

Exercise 4 invites you to focus on your interpersonal skill. People are some of the most valuable resources we have in our lives. It is so easy for everyone to get caught in their own patterns of thinking about themselves and about life. We also fall into habits and patterns that limit change. Interacting with people forces us to think new thoughts, to soften some of our habits, and to adapt to new challenges. The people in your life can be your greatest cheerleaders; rooting for your success. They can encourage you and pick you up when you are discouraged. They can share their resources and assistance with you when you are in need. When your life is eroding, it is easy to withdraw from some of the people you need to support and assist you. It is easy to take this resource for granted and so not use it to your best benefit.

TASK: Make a list of ten people you know who have been helpful to you in the past and/or are helpful to you now. Appreciate them as a resource that can help you move from hanging on by your fingernails to the next level of development, even if you don't yet know how to make them more useful.

SESSION 3

EXERCISE 1C – ACHIEVEMENT-STRIVING, ERODING

Session 3 introduces you to the concept of harnessing your energy and resources. You are eroding not necessarily because you lack adequate resources, but possibly because you aren't adequately harnessing the resources you possess. Let's get started.

Exercise 1 invites you to learn the skill of noticing your energy and resources. When you are struggling it is tempting to focus on the resources of others and to feel envious. You might find yourself saying to yourself that if you only had the resources and energy of your friend, you would be in a much better place than you are now. But, when you are paying attention to the energy and resources of your friend, you aren't seeing yours. It is time to start turning your attention toward yourself, and to begin taking stock of your own energy and resources.

TASK: See if you can catch yourself envying others for their resources and, if so, gently call your attention back to noticing your own.

EXERCISE 2C – ACHIEVEMENT-STRIVING, ERODING

Exercise 2 invites you to properly value your energy and resources. You may have a bias to assume that, even if you have some limited energy and resources, they are not adequate to effectively deal with the challenges and opportunities you are facing. That would be a natural assumption, since your life is eroding. But, this underestimation of your strengths makes it very difficult to harness their power. Sessions 1 and 2 should have opened your eyes to value your energy and resources more highly. But, that is only the beginning. You must learn to appreciate every manifestation of your energy and resources in order to see them as useful tools with which you can stop your decline and can build a satisfying and meaningful life.

TASK: Take out your list from Exercise 1 and read it through. Expand on it where you can. Notice skills and strengths that you have overlooked or haven't fully deployed.

EXERCISE 3C – ACHIEVEMENT-STRIVING, ERODING

Exercise 3 invites you to consider the value of sharpening your energy and your skills. Just as tools become less useful when they grow rusty and dull, your resources need constant attention if they are going to continue to be valuable and to grow in value. Envying the energy and resources of others diverts your attention from working with the skills you have. You have more than enough to solve your problems if you simply sharpen them. You sharpen them when you practice using them to address ordinary issues. The more you use them, the better you understand how they can be deployed to solve other problems and to address other issues.

TASK: Take out your list of skills and think through how you could use some of them to address issues you are facing today. Avoid thinking about what others can do to help you. Consider that you have all that you need if you only begin to use the gifts and skills you already possess.

EXERCISE 4C – ACHIEVEMENT-STRIVING, ERODING

Exercise 4 invites you to consider the value of expanding your energy and resources. Whatever positive energy and resources you currently have are only the foundation for what you can add. You simply can't afford to ignore your responsibility to cultivate and expand your positive energy and resources. The skills adequate to meet your needs today, won't be enough to meet your needs tomorrow. Life will continue to throw challenging circumstances your way in order to encourage you to expand your skills. You expand your skills when you take classes, start a new hobby, join a new club, learn a new skill, or make a new friend. Anything that stretches you, that requires you to do something new and different than what you have been doing will add to your resources. The fact that you are eroding suggests the need to add more skills to your toolbox.

TASK: Make a list of five ways you can expand your skills. Pick one and get to work.

SESSION 4
EXERCISE 1D – ACHIEVEMENT-STRIVING, ERODING

Session 4 invites you to focus your attention on ways you can begin to better deploy your energy and skills to create more positive results in your life. You see others using their resources better than you, and can now turn what you are learning from them into valuable changes in your life. It is of little value to have skills and resources that you aren't using. Exercise 1 invites you to learn the value of determined outcomes. Your life is eroding because there are issues depleting your life that you aren't addressing and solving. It is like a balloon that is gradually deflating because it has a few small holes that haven't yet been patched. Your life won't get much better until you identify one of those holes that you intend to patch. This requires taking responsibility for your life and intentionality to fix it. Until you identify one issue, you will passively watch your life continue to deflate.

TASK: Make a list of three to five issues that are currently deflating your life and need to be addressed. Which would you take on first?

EXERCISE 2D – ACHIEVEMENT-STRIVING, ERODING

Exercise 2 invited you to consider the skills required to make the change you need to make. In exercise 1, you identified one issue you want to fix. What resources do you need to fix it? If suddenly a tire went flat on your car, your progress would grind to a halt. You wouldn't be able to move forward until you repaired the flat. Once you decided to fix it, you would think through all of the things you would need: spare tire, jack, lug wrench. You might also consider your resources: Do I know how to use these things? If not, can I learn? Am I strong enough to change my tire? If not, who could I ask to help? This is an assessment of resources.

TASK: Now, apply this process to the issue you want to fix. What resources are required? Do you possess them? If not, where could you acquire them, and how would you do so?

EXERCISE 3D – ACHIEVEMENT-STRIVING, ERODING

Exercise 3 invites you to consider the energy required to make the changes you know you need to make. Let's go back to the story about the flat tire. You may want the tire to be fixed, but you simply don't have the "energy" to fix it. Instead, you would rather sit and wait for someone to come by and help. You don't think about the fact that you are wasting time and might be late for where you intended to go. The flat tire has given you an excuse to be passive. Or, you could harness your energy. You might decide that you don't want to be late because if you miss this interview, you might not get the job you really want. You might take pride in the fact that you can change your own tire or see changing the tire as a learning opportunity. Depending on how you choose to think about it, your energy will either rise or fall, grow or lessen.

TASK: Consider the issue you want to change. How can you think about the issue in a way that increases the energy necessary to fix it?

EXERCISE 4D – ACHIEVEMENT-STRIVING, ERODING

Exercise 4 invites you to consider the value of progressive expansion. Everything you learn creates a broader base to learn more. No experience is wasted. Everything you do adds to your resources and equips you to expand your resources further. Consider the flat tire. You could sit in your car and wait for someone to come by and fix it. If you make that choice, you have learned little. If, on the other hand, despite your concern that you aren't certain you can change your tire, you take it on, you have engaged in progressive expansion. You will need to figure out how to get the spare out of the trunk, to put the jack together, and to position it correctly under the car. You will learn how to loosen and tighten the lugs. You have just solved five or six problems you didn't know how to solve. That learning can be applied to many other issues that arise in your life. By changing the tire, you might take on an interest in replacing your brake pads. Your resources will expand steadily.

TASK: Write down one issue you have solved in your life. Next, list five to ten things you learned from solving that problem. Then, write one to two ways you have used those lessons to solve other problems. Amazing!

FACTOR – ACHIEVEMENT-STRIVING

This trait speaks to your ability to harness your energy and skills in a manner that can produce positive results. Those who have developed this skill are able to maximize their productivity. They use their time and resources judiciously and minimize wasted time and effort. Those who are low in this skill find themselves wishing for things to occur, procrastinating, and wasting time. They have difficulty getting their act together sufficiently to make things happen.

SELF-ASSESSED RATING – TREADING WATER

You are able to harness your energy and gifts successfully in the areas of your life that create stability and moderate success.

SESSION 1
EXERCISE 1A – ACHIEVEMENT-STRIVING, TREADING WATER

You are treading water largely because you know how to harness your energy and skills sufficiently to keep your life from eroding and yet, for a variety of reasons, have not been successful in doing so such that your life is growing. Clearly, you know what it means to harness your energy and skills—at least some of them. A football team is really two teams. One plays offense and is responsible for putting points on the board. The other plays defense and is charged with keeping the other team from scoring. Both are critical. You have built an effective defense that keeps your life from eroding. You know how to marshal your resources to that end, but you aren't as effective at doing so with the offensive part of your game. Session 1 will invite you to assess aspects of your energy and skill that are necessary to move forward. Let's get started.

Exercise 1 invites you to assess your physical energy. You might notice that you tend to have more energy when you are scared of things going bad than you have to make good things happen in your life.

TASK: Make a list of five things you don't want to happen in your life and five good things that would be improvements. For which list do you have more energy?

EXERCISE 2A – ACHIEVEMENT-STRIVING, TREADING WATER

Exercise 2 invites you to assess your level of mental energy to improve your life. Mental energy is evident when we anticipate things that can go wrong and when we envision things we want to create. Mental energy often precedes and directs our physical energy because it alerts us to potential threats and opportunities. People who are treading water often have more mental energy invested in anticipating things that can go wrong than they do in creating a preferred future. Reflect on your thoughts. Which seems to be predominant?

TASK: List ten of your most common and persistent thoughts. Now review the list. How many are about protecting what you have and how many are about creating something new and exciting?

EXERCISE 3A – ACHIEVEMENT-STRIVING, TREADING WATER

Exercise 3 invites you to consider the quality of your energy to make positive change. Your energy shows up as both negative and positive. Negative energy is filled with doubt, cynicism, and fear. It undermines taking action by suggesting that efforts to change will be a waste of time or too difficult to succeed. Positive energy works in the opposite way. It encourages you to take on challenges because it anticipates success and clearly sees the rewards and benefits of change.

TASK: Notice how your energy shifts when you are considering things that can go wrong in your life and when you imagine things you might want to create. Do you notice more positive energy when you take on solving a potential problem, and more negative energy when you think about taking on some project that is growth oriented?

EXERCISE 4A – ACHIEVEMENT-STRIVING, TREADING WATER

Exercise 4 invites you to consider the quality of your spiritual energy as a resource to create a better life. Spiritual energy shows up in your degree of belief that life is abundant enough for you to have whatever you want. If you have low spiritual energy it is likely that you will see yourself as lucky to have what you have, and to want more seems extreme, difficult, and excessive. You are willing to settle for a good life and not believe that you can have a wonderful one. High spiritual energy supports the idea that life has enough for everyone to have what they want and the only thing that limits us is our lack of vision and courage.

TASK: Rate your spiritual energy from 1 (low) to 5 (high). What limits your spiritual energy?

SESSION 2

EXERCISE 1B – ACHIEVEMENT-STRIVING, TREADING WATER

Session 2 focuses your attention on your skills and resources. It is critical that you notice and properly assess the resources you possess that are necessary to move your life from treading water to growing. You may have tools in your toolbox that you don't know you possess, or have not properly estimated their value or contemplated their use. Let's get started.

Exercise 1 invites you to focus on your education. Your education is a rich resource in your life and, perhaps, more so than you realize. It is likely that your education is one of the reasons your life is stable and secure. The data is clear that those who have a college education earn significantly more money than those who have only a high school education. Similarly, those who have earned an advanced degree earn more than those with a college education. Your education, regardless of extent, has opened many doors that you have used to secure your life.

TASK: Make a list of ten benefits you have received as a result of your education. What you likely don't clearly see is how much more benefit your education can bring to making your life better. Your education creates the foundation for further education. It qualifies you for new and different jobs. It has trained you in ways that are applicable beyond and above what you are doing now. List five ways you could use your education to improve your life.

EXERCISE 2B – ACHIEVEMENT-STRIVING, TREADING WATER

Exercise 2 invites you to focus on your experience. Experience, like education, is often underappreciated for its value and utility. Every experience in your life has expanded your knowledge, awareness, and depth. The work you do has taught you many more skills that have been directly applicable to your paycheck. You learned to work effectively with others. You learned how to work within a hierarchy. You learned hard skills and soft ones. In fact, your experience makes you more valuable than those with a similar education but without your level of experience.

TASK: Make a list of five assets that are the direct result of your experience. What you might not see clearly is how your experience can further enrich your life. Perhaps you were asked to give a presentation at work, something you had never done. You worked on it, and practiced, and then discovered you were pretty good at speaking to a group. Then, you just went back to work. But, you could have thought of other applications of that experience that could open new doors. Perhaps you could become a trainer at work and take on an entirely different role. Or, you could begin a career in public speaking or take on a political office. Your experience is very useful. List five new opportunities your experience could provide you.

EXERCISE 3B – ACHIEVEMENT-STRIVING, TREADING WATER

Exercise 3 invites you to focus on your self-care. This is a skill you have likely mastered. You are good at taking care of yourself and those people that are important to you. You set goals for your life and have reached most of them. You are relatively satisfied with the life you have built for yourself. However, the one part of your self-care you may have neglected is your care for your potential. Perhaps you have settled for less than you could have, and for being less than who you could be. Your success may mask the willingness to accept mediocrity rather than fostering and caring for your underlying potential. Here you may not have fully harnessed your care for yourself.

TASK: Make a list of five dreams you have had in your life that you have not fulfilled. Are you content to leave these goals undone?

EXERCISE 4B – ACHIEVEMENT-STRIVING, TREADING WATER

Exercise 4 invites you to focus on your interpersonal skills. People are one of your most valuable resources. Your friends and family have been instrumental in supporting your growth and success. Your parents helped you with your homework and pushed you to study hard. Your buddies told you about job opportunities that opened where they worked and put in a good word for you. Your family encouraged you to apply for the new role at work and to ask for a promotion. People have supported and encouraged you through your life journey and have helped you reach your level of success.

TASK: List five times you can recall being supported and/or encouraged by people in your life. What happened? Why have they stopped pushing you to reach for more? Perhaps you have collected people in your life who are accepting of your current level of success, or perhaps you have stopped listening to the push of your friends and family. Make a list of five people in your life who want you to reach for more and the things they are encouraging you to do.

SESSION 3
EXERCISE 1C – ACHIEVEMENT-STRIVING, TREADING WATER

Session 3 introduces you to the concept of harnessing your energy and resources. In Sessions 1 and 2 you became more aware of resources you might have overlooked. Now that you see them more clearly, you can focus on harnessing them to advance your life beyond treading water. Let's get started.

Exercise 1 invites you to better harness your energy and resources by simply noticing them more often. Because you are fairly content with your life, the energy and resources you need to make improvements may be overlooked simply because you have had no need of them. Why would you consider what you know about gardening if you never plan to plant a garden? But, when you notice your resources, you might also find more motivation to make positive changes. You may not realize how equipped you are to make your life even better.

TASK: List five resources you possess but aren't currently using.

EXERCISE 2C – ACHIEVEMENT-STRIVING, TREADING WATER

Exercise 2 invites you to properly value your energy and resources. Not only may you have been overlooking some of your unused resources, you are also likely to have been undervaluing them. It is only when you are trying to build something that you truly value the tools in your toolbox. It is only when you are trying to make some change in your life that you come to properly value the skills and experiences you have that allow you to make that change.

TASK: Take out your list from Exercise 1. How could you use your resources to make positive changes in your life? If you fully used them, what could you do?

EXERCISE 3C – ACHIEVEMENT-STRIVING, TREADING WATER

Exercise 3 invites you to consider the value of sharpening your energy and skills. You may have heard of the book entitled *What Got You Here Won't Get You There*. The point is that the skills and effort needed to get you to your current level of success aren't sufficient to move you on beyond that point. And, that is often the case. It is also true that the energy and skills you possess require attention and care if they are to continue to be as useful to you now as they were in the past. No one can afford to stay where they are. You are either moving forward or sliding backward, because life is always changing and it requires that you keep up.

TASK: List five skills that have been especially useful to you. Write down what you have done to sharpen or cultivate them in the past 12 months. What could you take on to make them more useful?

EXERCISE 4C – ACHIEVEMENT-STRIVING, TREADING WATER

Exercise 4 invites you to consider the value of expanding your energy and resources. As pointed out in exercise 3 the skills that helped you get to your current level of success must always be honed and sharpened lest they fall into disrepair and become less useful. It is also true that your resources must be constantly expanded. In order to get your life to the place where you are growing, you will need to learn new skills, take on new challenges, and harness your energy. There is always a "very next step" on every journey. It is always the most important one because it is the one we need to take.

TASK: List two new skills you could learn in order to take your very next step.

SESSION 4
EXERCISE 1D – ACHIEVEMENT-STRIVING, TREADING WATER

Session 4 asks you to focus your attention on ways you can begin to deploy your energy and skills to move beyond treading water and toward growing. You know how to build a satisfying life for yourself but aren't applying all of your resources toward growing. You are making yourself satisfied with a good life rather than pressing on for a better one; at least not the best one you could have. Let's get started.

Exercise 1 invites you to more highly value a preferred state. There have been times in your past when you were discontented and wanted more for your life. At those times, you envisioned what you wanted and then harnessed your energy and resources to get what you wanted. Now, for some reason you stopped dreaming for more and made yourself content. We are inviting you to dream again. Sometimes when life is good it is difficult to dream for more.

TASK: List five things you would like for your life that you don't have. Don't be practical and don't hold back.

EXERCISE 2D – ACHIEVEMENT-STRIVING, TREADING WATER

Exercise 2 invites you to consider the skills required to reach the dreams you listed in Exercise 1. In the past, you took stock of your skills before you took on a growth challenge. You wanted to buy a home and you considered your resources; your savings, you income, the amount you could borrow. You wanted a better job and considered your background, education, and contacts that could make introductions. Assessing your resources helps you understand if you have enough of what you need to get where you want to go. It is the first step in moving forward. If you have what you need, you are ready now. If you don't, you will need to add to your skills.

TASK: Take one of your dreams from Exercise 1 and list the resources you currently possess that would be useful in reaching that goal.

EXERCISE 3D – ACHIEVEMENT-STRIVING, TREADING WATER

Exercise 3 invites you to consider the energy required to move from treading water to growing. Your current situation is pretty good. It doesn't require a great deal of energy or effort to stay where you are. Growing will require more of both. You will need to learn some new skills, put out extra effort and get out of your comfort zone. The best way to harness your energy is to become excited and hopeful about your future. The more you envision the benefit you will get from reaching your goals, the more your energy will be available to you.

TASK: Use your dream from Exercise 2. Take ten minutes to imagine how your life will be better and how you will feel when you have achieved it. Let the joy and excitement motivate you.

EXERCISE 4D – ACHIEVEMENT-STRIVING, TREADING WATER

Exercise 4 invites you to consider the value of growing over treading water. Life is constantly changing. Unless you are changing and growing, it is likely that you are falling behind. Your skills are getting stale. You are becoming content and lazy. You are allowing your life to get out of shape and flabby. Growing is a perpetual workout for your life. It requires shifting into learning mode. It demands that you become flexible. It stretches your courage and your appetite for adventure and change. Growing brings significant benefit to your life beyond the concrete expansion of achieving new dreams.

TASK: Think of times in the past when you have been growing and list five benefits from being in that mindset.

FACTOR – ACHIEVEMENT-STRIVING

This trait speaks to your ability to harness your energy and skills in a manner that can produce positive results. Those who have developed this skill are able to maximize their productivity. They use their time and resources judiciously and minimize wasted time and effort. Those who are low in this skill find themselves wishing for things to occur, procrastinating and wasting time. They have difficulty getting their act together sufficiently to make things happen.

SELF-ASSESSED RATING – GROWING

You are able to harness your energy and gifts in ways that allow you to grow and expand your life but with some limitations.

SESSION 1
EXERCISE 1A – ACHIEVEMENT-STRIVING, GROWING

You are growing largely because you have learned how to effectively harness your energy and skills to advance your life. However, it is likely that you have some gaps; some places where you either aren't fully aware of your resources or aren't harnessing them to their fullest potential. The following exercises are designed to assist you in exploring how you can even more fully harness your energy and skills to produce the very best life you can have. Session 1 encourages you to assess aspects of your energy and skills that might not currently be fully harnessed. Let's get started.

Exercise 1 invites you to assess your physical energy. Growing requires having your physical energy engaged much of the time. You can't produce the quality of life you are living sitting on the couch all day or wasting a lot of time day dreaming. You are a person of action. However, if you assess your life carefully, you might find times and/or places where you are coasting or wasting time. There is likely a reason for this that we will explore later.

TASK: Review your schedule for the past week. Write down any occurrences when you were wasting time or simply drifting.

EXERCISE 2A – ACHIEVEMENT-STRIVING, GROWING

Exercise 2 invites you to assess the full engagement of your mental energy. Mental energy is evident in how we are intellectually engaged in our world. Your mental energy is engaged when you are envisioning your future, identifying opportunities and obstacles, solving problems, being creative, planning, assessing, adjusting, and celebrating. Mental energy is wasted when you are numbing out watching television, playing video games, drinking, doing drugs or participating in other activities that allow you to coast rather than to engage. It isn't likely that you are wasting a lot of mental energy but you might have times, places or relationships where you do.

TASK: Make a list of all of the times in the last week where you were mentally coasting. What were you doing during those times?

EXERCISE 3A – ACHIEVEMENT-STRIVING, GROWING

Exercise 3 invites you to consider the quality of your energy. You are used to living, for the most part, in positive energy. Positive energy is focused on making changes, getting things done, moving forward, solving problems, and healthy interpersonal relations. You know the power of positive energy to get things done and to build alliances. But, you may have a few places or a few relationships where your energy slips toward negativity. Focus on places where you are cynical, skeptical, and negative, and on people with whom you are a bit passive-aggressive. These small gaps in positive energy are likely contributing to the fact that you aren't yet fully thriving.

TASK: Make a list of any of these relationships or places where you have less than full positive energy.

EXERCISE 4A – ACHIEVEMENT-STRIVING, GROWING

Exercise 4 invites you to consider the quality of your spiritual energy to move toward thriving. Spiritual energy refers to your belief that life is abundant and that there is more than enough for you to have whatever you want without taking from others. Sometimes it is a gap in spiritual energy that limits thriving. You may feel so grateful for the goodness in your life that you don't believe you have a right to have more. Expanding your spiritual energy allows you to expand your dreams for all that can be possible, and to see how your life can have an even bigger impact on the world around you.

TASK: List three strengths and three weaknesses in your spiritual energy.

SESSION 2
EXERCISE 1B – ACHIEVEMENT-STRIVING, GROWING

Session 2 focuses your attention on your skills and resources. You are certainly aware of many, if not most, of your skills, but thriving may require some of which you may not be fully aware or may not be fully deploying. You have amazing potential, much more than you are likely to be utilizing. Let's get started.

Exercise 1 invites you to focus on your education. Your formal and informal education is a rich and valuable resource to use for thriving. Not only have you learned many facts about the world and life, you have also learned to stretch, to question, to grow, to think, and to dream through your schooling. Consider the great people whose lives you have studied. Is not each of them a model for thriving? Are they not great because they didn't settle for simply growing, but pressed beyond those borders for even more? Don't their lives provide models for you to follow?

TASK: List five lessons you have learned through your education that could help you move toward thriving.

EXERCISE 2B – ACHIEVEMENT-STRIVING, GROWING

Exercise 2 invites you to focus on your experience. You have a wealth of experiences every day that actually encourage you to push toward thriving. Since you are growing, you know how to recognize opportunity and to step into challenges.

You experience the benefit of situations that require you to become flexible, to learn, to change, and to grow. And, you see that you have the ability to master almost every challenge you have faced. That is how you have been able to grow. One lesson you can extract from your experience is that you probably could take on more. If you are mastering almost all of your challenges, it is likely you are taking on ones worthy of your ability. Perhaps you should press for more until you reach those that you can't do. That would be the limit of your ability.

TASK: Write down three challenges that are beyond what you are doing now, but might be worthy of your life.

EXERCISE 3B – ACHIEVEMENT-STRIVING, GROWING

Exercise 3 invites you to focus on your self-care. Caring for yourself is a critical skill for everyone. The better you take care of yourself, the more you have to offer those around you. You can't be growing as you are without having become skillful at self-care. But, there may be some gaps in how and where you are caring for yourself. You have one or two bad habits that undermine what is the very best for you. You may have one or two relationships that aren't sufficiently challenging, encouraging, or positive. You may know you need to make changes in a few areas to improve your self-care, but have been unwilling to do so.

TASK: List any ways you aren't taking the best care of yourself? Are you willing to make changes?

EXERCISE 4B – ACHIEVEMENT-STRIVING, GROWING

Exercise 4 invites you to focus on your interpersonal skills. Thriving requires the ability to interact with others in the most positive and constructive manner. It requires the ability to be deeply and genuinely concerned for the welfare of the people you meet and to form win/win relationships wherever you go. Harnessing your interpersonal skills for thriving requires a loss of the ego such that you don't see yourself as needing to compete with anyone, and don't compare yourself to others in order to derive your sense of significance. It is likely you are skilled in many ways, but may have some work in harnessing some underdeveloped interpersonal skills.

TASK: List three ways you could expand interpersonally.

SESSION 3
EXERCISE 1C – ACHIEVEMENT-STRIVING, GROWING

Session 3 introduces you to the concept of harnessing your energy and resources. In Sessions 1 and 2 you became more aware of resources you possess but may not be applying to some of the more challenging areas you are currently facing. Now that you see your resources more clearly and appraise them more accurately, you are better prepared to apply them to the few remaining issues that keep you from fully thriving. Let's get started.

Exercise 1 invites you to better harness your energy and resources by simply noticing where you aren't using them fully. Since you are used to using your resources effectively, if you are willing, you should be able to see pretty clearly where you are holding back or avoiding the full application of your skills and abilities.

TASK: Simply notice and make a list of those areas or relationships.

EXERCISE 2C – ACHIEVEMENT-STRIVING, GROWING

Exercise 2 invites you to consider the reason you aren't fully applying your resources to those few areas that are holding you back. This is an important step of growth. You may have some fear about the consequences of moving forward that is rooted in your history. For example, your parents may have divorced and you fear that the full utilization of your resources will threaten the security of your marriage. Consider what might cause you to hold back and not use all of your resources.

TASK: Write down whatever comes to mind. Then, look at the list. Is anything on your list more important than the full expression of your life? Be honest. If the answer is yes, you know you aren't quite ready to thrive. You have some sacred cows that are more important to you than your life.

EXERCISE 3C – ACHIEVEMENT-STRIVING, GROWING

Exercise 3 invites you to consider if you have any upper limits issues that are hampering your ability to harness all of your resources. Your success and the goodness of your life may have exceeded all of your expectations. You may be on the upper limit of your comfort zone, and are having difficulty accepting any more opportunity, power, happiness, or love into your life. You may have been here before, and found that you sabotage your success when it became too great. Until you expand your upper limit, you won't allow yourself to fully use your gifts and abilities.

TASK: Review your life and see if there is a pattern of stopping or sabotaging your success when it became uncomfortable for you. If so, you have some work to do visualizing your expanded success and becoming more comfortable with it before you can go on.

EXERCISE 4C – ACHIEVEMENT-STRIVING, GROWING

Exercise 4 invites you to consider the value of breaking through into full thriving. Your life is very good. You have much to be proud of and content with. There is no need to reach for more. But...if life can be this good, how much better might it still be? Perhaps instead of making yourself content with your growing life, you should take your success as if it is only a milestone toward much more.

TASK: Take some time to appreciate all that you have. Now consider multiplying it times two or three or four. Imagine your life that much better. Write down what comes to mind. Use this image to motivate yourself to use your energy and resources to break through those remaining few barriers.

SESSION 4

EXERCISE 1D – ACHIEVEMENT-STRIVING, GROWING

Session 4 asks you to focus your attention on applying your energy and skills such that you break through the few barriers that keep you from thriving. In Session 3 you identified those obstacles and considered how much better your life would be if you took them on. Let's get started.

Exercise 1 invites you to consider your one or two last "bad habits" that must be sacrificed in order for you to thrive. You have done a great job growing your life, but you may have held on to one or two indulgencies that limit the full harnessing of your resources.

TASK: As soon as you read this, if something comes immediately to mind, you should write it down. Your subconscious mind knows exactly what you need to give up in order to move on.

EXERCISE 2D – ACHIEVEMENT-STRIVING, GROWING

Exercise 2 invites you to consider your next big opportunity. Thriving comes only by growing. Growing requires taking on something new and different; something with which you may not have experience or confidence. Thriving requires some sort of transformation for how you are being in the world. You don't need to chart out your ten year course. You need only to identify the immediate challenge before you. What is the one thing you should be taking on right now in order to thrive? This may not immediately come to your mind, but if you sit with the question for a while, it will show up. Perhaps there is a book you need to write that you have been putting off because you have never written a book. Or, some cause for you to take on, but it seems daunting and huge.

TASK: Write down that next big thing and begin marshaling your resources to take it on.

EXERCISE 3D – ACHIEVEMENT-STRIVING, GROWING

Exercise 3 invites you to consider that last remaining obstacle in your path toward thriving. You have done a great job of identifying and removing obstacles along your path, but that does not mean that you have removed them all. The fact that you are not fully thriving suggests the possibility that you have at least one obstacle holding you back. Where are you not fully being yourself? With whom are you pretending to be who you are not? Where are you not being fully honest and open? Any place where you are not fully being you is a place where you aren't fully utilizing your energy and resources. You are being less than you.

TASK: Write down whatever comes to mind and determine to take it on.

EXERCISE 4D – ACHIEVEMENT-STRIVING, GROWING

Exercise 4 invites you to have one or two fierce conversations. Fierce conversations are your opportunity to show up, speak your truth, and clear the air. They are your way of clearing up misunderstandings and creating correct understandings. They are your opportunity to leave behind whatever baggage you are carrying in order to thrive.

TASK: Take out your list from Exercise 3. Are there any people on that list with whom you need to have a "fierce conversation"? If so, write down the message you need to communicate to each person in order to break free and to move on. Now, schedule those conversations.

EXERCISE SERIES: ZEST

FACTOR – ZEST

Zest combined with enthusiasm, vigor, and vitality points to the energy you bring to life. Those who are high on this scale exude enthusiasm in all their pursuits. They are "gas pedals" for the world around them, advancing their plans, and getting things done with vigor. Those who are low on this scale manifest a lethargy that is difficult for them to overcome. Everything seems as if it requires more energy than they have available.

SELF-ASSESSED RATING – HANGING ON

You seem to have very little energy, vitality, and vigor with which to manage your life.

SESSION 1
EXERCISE 1A – ZEST, HANGING ON

One of the biggest reasons you are hanging on in your life is because you almost completely lack zest. You don't feel hardly any enjoyment or enthusiasm in your daily life. This might seem shocking to you. You may have grown so accustomed to the way you experience your life that it seems perfectly normal to experience no zest. The goal of these exercises is to wake you up so that you not only see your lack of enthusiasm, but you also understand the consequences of its absence. Let's get started.

Exercise 1 invites you to do a simple assessment.

TASK: How would you grade your zest on a 5-point scale? Give yourself a score of 1 if you have little to no zest, and a 5 if you exhibit a great deal of it. Now, check yourself by asking five people to grade you. Pick people who will be honest with you. Are you surprised with how they see you?

EXERCISE 2A – ZEST, HANGING ON

The following three exercises will focus only on the absence of enjoyment in your life; one of the two factors that determine zest. Enjoyment or happiness is powerful fuel that provides your life with vision, hope, and motivation that is critically important for making positive change. Without enjoyment, there are only three major emotions we can experience. Exercise 2 invites you to focus on sadness, the first of the three negative emotions. Sadness is simply the absence of enjoyment or joy. To the extent your predominant emotion is sadness, you will have low energy, little enthusiasm, and minimal interest in life. It is as if you have no gas in your tank. Without enjoyment to fuel change, you are at the mercy of the gravitational pull of life toward chaos and dysfunction. It is like having a garden but having no energy to tend to it. Before long it will be overwhelmed with weeds and will be of no value.

TASK: Rate your level of unhappiness from 1 (extremely unhappy) to 5 (not unhappy at all).

EXERCISE 3A – ZEST, HANGING ON

Exercise 3 invites you to focus on anger, the second of the three negative emotions. Anger is the result of judgments that you aren't being treated fairly, that others are at fault, and that you deserve better circumstances and opportunities than those you have. Anger creates problems in two ways. First, it justifies doing nothing to improve your situation because it focuses your attention on what others should be doing instead of on what you can do for yourself. It is like waiting to be rescued, rather than swimming to shore. The second negative effect of anger is that it drives people away from you. It is difficult to be around someone who is always angry. Instead of inviting people into your world as potential assets, you will isolate yourself.

TASK: Rate your level of anger from 1 (extremely angry) to 5 (not angry at all).

EXERCISE 4A – ZEST, HANGING ON

Exercise 4 invites you to focus on fear, the third of the three negative emotions. Fear is the result of seeing yourself as the victim of forces greater than yourself.

It causes you to see yourself as helpless, at the mercy of your circumstances, and unable to do anything to effect positive change. The result of fear is paralysis, or the inability to move in any direction to make something good happen. Fear will sap you of any thoughts or actions that could make your life better.

TASK: Rate your level of fear from 1 (extremely fearful) to 5 (not fearful at all).

SESSION 2
EXERCISE 1B – ZEST, HANGING ON

The second aspect of zest is enthusiasm. Enthusiasm is defined as an absorbing or controlling possession of the mind by any interest or pursuit; lively interest. While enjoyment or joy is emotional, enthusiasm in mental. It is about actively engaging your mind with your life. Enthusiasm keeps you engaged in understanding your world, identifying obstacles, and creatively solving problems. Low enthusiasm shows up in passive acceptance, as if there is nothing you can do to effect change in your life.

Exercise 1 invites you to notice your level of enthusiasm.

TASK: Rate yourself on your degree of enthusiasm from 1 (no enthusiasm) to 5 (a great deal of enthusiasm).

EXERCISE 2B – ZEST, HANGING ON

Enthusiasm has three components, apathy lethargy, and passivity. The better you understand the reasons your life is in decline, the better equipped you are to reverse course. Let's start with the first. Exercise 2 invites you to notice your level of apathy. Apathy is the absence of caring about yourself and your life. You are apathetic when you stop caring about the cleanliness and neatness of your home and accept things being broken, cluttered, and dirty. You are apathetic when you stop caring about what you eat and drink, and make yourself content eating food that requires no effort to prepare and offers little or no nutrition, but is cheap and quick. You are apathetic when you stop caring about your appearance and put no effort in your hygiene, clothing, or grooming. Apathy is giving up on the quality of your life.

TASK: Rate your level of apathy from 1 (completely apathetic) to 5 (not apathetic at all).

EXERCISE 3B – ZEST, HANGING ON

Exercise 3 invites you to notice your level of lethargy; the second component of zest. Lethargy is the absence of action. You may actually care about your declining circumstances but are too lethargic to do anything about it. Lethargy is a bit like laziness; it is the inability to rally sufficient energy to get anything done. You may wake up in the morning with great intentions of all you plan to get done, but at the end of the day notice that nothing on your list was accomplished. Or, you might sit down to read a book or learn something new, only to find that you drift off to sleep or procrastinate by watching television. For whatever reason, you are watching your life decline in front of your eyes, but seem unable to do anything about it. If these things are true of you, you are suffering from lethargy.

TASK: Rate your level of lethargy from 1 (extremely lethargic) to 5 (not lethargic at all).

EXERCISE 4B – ZEST, HANGING ON

Exercise 4 invites you to notice your level of passivity; the third component of zest. Passivity is the acceptance of what is occurring without any resistance or effort to change. Passivity sometimes results from the experience of not finding ways to exert positive control over negative circumstances. If such a situation persists over time, it may result in passive acceptance of whatever is occurring, both good and bad. You are passive if you get your credit card bill in the mail and either don't open it or just throw it in the trash. You are passive when you get notified that your power company is going to cut off service and you do nothing.

Passivity is the ultimate form of giving up; giving up responsibility for your own welfare and for the management of your life.

TASK: Rate your level of passivity from 1 (extremely passive) to 5 (not passive at all).

SESSION 3
EXERCISE 1C – ZEST, HANGING ON

Session 3 focuses your attention on the internal implications of having little zest for your life. Internal implications are the effect low zest has on your thinking, feeling, beliefs, and actions. These are critical because they interact together in shaping your life. Your thoughts create your feelings. Your feelings and beliefs will largely determine your actions. Let's get started.

Exercise 1 invites you to notice the impact of your low zest on your pattern of thinking. Low zest will narrow the focus and scope of your thinking. Instead of thinking bigger thoughts and exploring expanding concerns, low zest will result in noticing only what is brought to your attention. You will have less curiosity, creativity, and openness to new ideas. You will find yourself having fewer interests and being preoccupied with repetitive thoughts and ideas. Constricted thinking makes it more difficult for you to even see changes you need to make.

TASK: Make a list of ten of your most frequent thoughts. Notice how often you think those thoughts, and how long you have been thinking about them without making any change.

EXERCISE 2C – ZEST, HANGING ON

Exercise 2 invites you to notice the impact of your low zest on your feelings about your life. Feelings range between very optimistic and hopeful, to very pessimistic and despairing. Low zest over a long period of time results in more pessimistic and despairing feelings. You may experience yourself feeling hopeless, as if trying to change is a waste of time. Or, your feelings may be dominated by resentment and bitterness that provides you with excuses as to why your life is as it is. Hopeless feelings make it very difficult to even contemplate a better situation.

TASK: List your five most predominant and pervasive feelings. Ask three friends or family members if they agree with your list. Consider the implications of such negative feelings in creating your current state of affairs.

EXERCISE 3C – ZEST, HANGING ON

Exercise 3 invites you to notice the impact of your low zest on your beliefs about your life. Beliefs contribute strongly to the strength or weakness of your life because your beliefs shape your expectations. If you believe you can have an amazingly successful and satisfying life, you are highly more likely to achieve it than if you have no such belief. It is also true that if you believe you will never and can never have a happy and rich life, that belief easily becomes a self-fulfilling prophesy. Hence, understanding and taking responsibility for your beliefs about your life is critical to managing it.

TASK: Take the next 30 minutes and write down your beliefs about your life. Write down whatever comes to mind about what you believe you can have with regards to money, security, love, success, recognition, acceptance, significance, and meaning. Notice how your beliefs have been shaping your life to this point. Now, consider how your beliefs will continue to shape your life if you don't change them.

EXERCISE 4C – ZEST, HANGING ON

Exercise 4 invites you to notice the impact of your low zest on your activity and level of action. Low zest usually results in a low level of activity and action. It is almost as if your low zest has slowed you down to a crawl. You don't have the energy you used to have. You get tired out and exhausted easily. Even the most simple task can be taxing and drain you of whatever little energy you have. Having such low energy and activity makes it almost impossible to make changes, especially if they are big and complex. Your minimal action makes it difficult to accomplish anything.

TASK: Notice your level of activity. What did you accomplish yesterday? The day before? Today? Are you surprised by how little activity you now have in your life? Can you recall when you got a lot more accomplished in a day?

SESSION 4

EXERCISE 1D – ZEST, HANGING ON

Session 4 focuses your attention on the external implications of having little zest. All positive change starts with changes you make within yourself, but the impact of those changes is seen in the world around you. If you are to take full responsibility for your life, you must accept the results your low zest is creating in your life. Let's get started.

Exercise 1 invites you to notice how your expectations for your life have diminished. Most children have big and ambitious expectations for their lives. They envision being doctors, teachers, or astronauts. Those expectations pushed them to take on challenges and to overcome obstacles. Your low zest has eroded your expectations such that you may have difficulty even imagining your life being substantially better. It may be as if you have become accustomed to losing and so now can't imagine a win. Low expectations greatly shape low outcomes. Until you expand your expectations for your life, it will be severely limited.

TASK: List five expectations you currently have for your life. Do they feel big enough? Try taking each and expanding it dramatically. See if you can imagine a much better outcome.

EXERCISE 2D – ZEST, HANGING ON

Exercise 2 invites you to notice how your low zest has caused you to withdraw from life. In life you have to play to win. To the extent you retreat from playing, you are less likely to win. Low zest frequently leads to a slow pattern of withdraw and inactivity. You may often find yourself saying that you don't have the energy to go out in the evening with friends. You may not have enough enthusiasm to apply for a better job. You might not be able to muster the motivation to go to the gym or even the grocery store. Withdrawing can happen so subtly that you don't even notice the decline, much less take responsibility for the outcome.

TASK: Review your life over the past three years. What activities are you currently engaged in? Are you engaged in more activities now than in years past, or is the opposite true? an you see that if you continue the pattern of withdrawing from life, it will only lead to further loss and decay?

EXERCISE 3D – ZEST, HANGING ON

Exercise 3 invites you to notice how your low zest has resulted in isolation. This might seem obvious or it may not. Your withdrawal has an impact on those around you. While people may notice that you aren't as engaged in life as you used to be, and so reach out to you and attempt to keep you involved, eventually they will grow weary of putting out the effort. You will find yourself more and more isolated. Your social circle will shrink and eventually disappear. You will find fewer people with whom to interact, to share dreams, to expand your flexibility, and to challenge your limitations. Isolation leaves you alone with the negative patterns you have developed. There are fewer friends whose lives can show you a more functional and healthy way to live. There are fewer people to encourage you to get back in the game. You are creating your own island on which you live by yourself. While that might make your life easier, it won't make it richer.

TASK: Make a list of your current friends. Has the list grown over the past three years or gotten smaller? Are you as involved with your friends as you used to be, or are you less involved? What will happen to you if you continue to isolate yourself?

EXERCISE 4D – ZEST, HANGING ON

Exercise 4 invites you to notice how your low zeal leads to rejection and decline. Whether you face it or not, your life is either getting stronger or getting weaker. Whether you like it or not, you are either winning the game of life or losing it. Winning tends to be attractive others. People like to be around a winner; to learn from their wisdom and to share in the benefits of their victories. At the same time, people don't tend to like being around a loser. They have little to offer and are often unpleasant in their attitude. You may not like thinking of yourself as a loser, but your life is evidence that you are headed in that direction. You might hope that things will magically turn around but that rarely happens and is a misplaced hope. The turnaround will come when you see where you are and when you take responsibility for all that is happening to you. You are the captain of this ship. Its welfare and success are your job! Are you a winner or a loser? You get to decide.

TASK: Write down which word best describes you now? Now, write down who you want to be.

FACTOR – ZEST

Zest combined with Enthusiasm, Vigor and Vitality point to the energy you bring to life. Those who are high on this scale exude enthusiasm in all their pursuits. They are "gas pedals" for the world around them, advancing their plans and getting things done with vigor. Those who are low on this scale manifest a lethargy that is difficult for them to overcome. Everything seems as if it requires more energy than they have available.

SELF-ASSESSED RATING – ERODING

Your energy, vitality, and vigor have been declining and you lack the ability to halt the decline.

SESSION 1

EXERCISE 1A – ZEST, ERODING

Your life is eroding largely because you lack sufficient zest to address the challenges and to take advantage of the opportunities you are currently encountering in your life. Zest is liveliness or energy. It is the fuel that powers your life. Without sufficient fuel you will be overwhelmed by life. Session 1 focuses your attention on aspects of zest which you need to become aware. Until you can see the issues that undermine you, it will be difficult to address them. Let's get started.

Exercise 1 invites you to notice your vitality. Vitality can be defined as your capacity for survival or for the continuation of a meaningful or purposeful existence. You might think of vitality as your expectation for your life. If you believe you should have a richer and more meaningful life, you will work harder to attain it. If, on the other hand, you have low vitality, you are likely to have low expectations and so are unwilling to exert much effort to make things better.

TASK: How would you rate your vitality from 1 (very low) to 5 (very high)? What evidence supports your rating?

EXERCISE 2A – ZEST, ERODING

Exercise 2 invites you to consider the second aspect of zest which is vigor. Vigor is your force of healthy growth. Think of vigor as that spark inside you that seeks to make your life better. It is almost an innate force that operates in all of us to press us to move forward. Perhaps you can recall when your vigor was high. You felt alive and were actively shaping your life. You seemed to have a great deal of energy to take risks and try new things. Perhaps now your vigor is low. You find yourself a bit lethargic and without much drive to change.

TASK: Rate your level of vigor from 1 (very low) to 5 (very high). Why has your vigor diminished?

EXERCISE 3A – ZEST, ERODING

Exercise 3 invites you to consider the third aspect of zest which is enthusiasm. Enthusiasm is absorbing or controlling possession of the mind by any interest or pursuit; lively interest. When you have high enthusiasm your mind is active and engaged in the world around you. You find yourself interested in all kinds of new and different things. You are naturally curious and open to learn. When your enthusiasm is low, the opposite is the case. You don't seem to have that much interest in anything. You tend to gravitate to the familiar and to fall into ruts and habit patterns. You don't have many new thoughts and get caught up in repetitive thinking.

TASK: Rate your level of enthusiasm from 1 (very low) to 5 (very high). How is low enthusiasm limiting your life?

EXERCISE 4A – ZEST, ERODING

Exercise 4 invites you to consider the final aspect of zest, which is low energy. Life is not easy for anyone. It constantly provides opportunities and challenges that require your engagement. When you have low energy you lack the interest and ability to do what needs to be done. You gradually become more of a passive observer of your life; noticing opportunities to make your life better, but lacking the energy to get involved. It is like watching your life gradually slip through your fingers while lacking the energy to close them. It is a helpless and hopeless feeling.

TASK: Rate your level of energy from 1 (low energy) to 5 (high energy). Hopefully, you are beginning to see the ways your low zest is negatively impacting your life.

SESSION 2
EXERCISE 1B – ZEST, ERODING

Session 2 will focus your attention on some of the implications of having insufficient zest. Clearly, it is taking a toll on your life. Understanding how low zest is causing your life to erode is a necessary step in reversing the trend. Let's get started.

Exercise 1 invites you to focus on excessive acceptance of your life as it currently exists. A successful and happy life is built on the desire to have more. When you want a better marriage, more money, a closer relationship with your children, or to be in great shape, you lay the foundation for improvement. Acceptance undermines your life by making it okay to be where you are and to have what you possess. Acceptance robs you of your drive to have more. Do a thorough assessment of your life as it currently exists.

TASK: List all of the areas where you are accepting your circumstances and know you should want more. Review your list every day for the next week and add to it.

EXERCISE 2B – ZEST, ERODING

Exercise 2 invites you to focus on low engagement and its impact on your eroding life. It is not enough to simply want a better life. Making improvements requires getting involved. Your life won't magically improve. Things won't stop eroding and start improving until you get engaged. Low zest often results in low engagement. You may have noticed that you are less involved in life than you used to be. More and more you are watching life happen to you instead of being involved in shaping it. You must get involved if your life is going to get better. You are either getting more engaged or becoming less engaged in shaping your life. Which is the case for you?

TASK: List five ways you have become less engaged in shaping your life. Now, list five ways you could become more engaged.

EXERCISE 3B – ZEST, ERODING

Exercise 3 invites you to focus on the amount of effort you expend in shaping your life. Engagement is good but not sufficient to stop eroding and start making positive changes. Low zest almost always results in low effort. It is rarely enough to make one attempt to solve a problem to take advantage of one opportunity. Often, life requires sustained and/or repeated effort in order to achieve your outcome. When you make one try, don't succeed, and then give up, you set yourself up for further erosion. Insufficient effort is one of the main reasons people fail to create for themselves the success they desire.

TASK: List five goals you failed to achieve due to insufficient effort.

EXERCISE 4B – ZEST, ERODING

Exercise 4 invites you to consider the pattern you are creating for yourself due to low zest. Failure isn't always bad. In fact, you can learn some lessons from failure that can't easily be learned through success, but repeated failure begins to create a pattern from which it can be difficult to escape. Insufficient zest will set you up for failure after failure, which puts you at risk for seeing yourself as a failure and giving up on the idea that your life can get better. Once you reach the point of hopelessness, you are in real trouble. It is so very important to create some wins, even small ones, and to use those wins to fuel your hope and enthusiasm to have more.

TASK: Make a list of five wins you have created over the past year. They don't have to be big. Use them to feed your dream for your future. If you could succeed there, you can succeed anywhere.

SESSION 3
EXERCISE 1C – ZEST, ERODING

One of the strengths that distinguish you from those who are hanging on by their fingernails is that you can observe healthy behavior in those around you and can learn from their successes. You have not become so discouraged as to think that things can't get better for you. Your ability to model helpful behavior is a very real asset. In Session 3 your attention is focused on four skills that the successful people you know have mastered and from which you can strengthen your life. Let's get started.

Exercise 1 invites you to focus on the power of belief to impact zest. Pick one of your friends or family members whose life is in better shape than yours at this point. Note one thing they have that you would like for your life. Notice that they believe they have the right to be successful in that area. If they have more money than you, notice that they believe they can have that much money. They don't think it is impossible or lucky. They believe there is a clear pathway to have what they want. You need to harness the power of belief in your life.

TASK: Pick one thing you want very much. Write it down. Imagine that you possess it now. What does it feel like to have it? Visualize this every day for the next week to feed your zest.

EXERCISE 2C – ZEST, ERODING

Exercise 2 invites you to focus on the necessity of high engagement in shaping your life. Again, pick someone you know who is successful in some way that you want for your life. What do they have or what have they accomplished that you want? What did they do to achieve that goal?

TASK: Make a list. If you aren't certain, meet with them and ask what they did to get where they are. Ask them to be specific and to give you all of the steps. You need to come to see the level of engagement that is required to get what you want. You may have no idea how involved you need to be in order to reach your goals. Sometimes it seems the path is so clear and straightforward when, in fact, it is much longer and more complex. Now, take an area of your life that is eroding. How would you need to be engaged in order to stop the erosion?

EXERCISE 3C – ZEST, ERODING

Exercise 3 invites you to focus on the energy required to persevere through to success. Pick another friend or family member whose life is growing and not eroding. They are doing a better job managing their life than you are. The same forces that operate on your life operate on theirs, but they have managed them better.

TASK: Pick one area of their life where they are doing better than you are. Write it down. How much energy have they been expending to create the success they are experiencing? How hard have they worked to get where they are? How much effort did they expend to overcome the opposition and problems they faced? Learn from their example. Your life won't stop eroding until you muster the energy necessary not only to engage life but to persevere through the challenges.

EXERCISE 4C – ZEST, ERODING

Exercise 4 invites you to focus on positive outcomes and their impact on zest. Pick a friend or family member whose life is growing or thriving. They have done quite well for themselves and not only are successful but seem quite happy and satisfied with their life.

TASK: Make a list of their successes. If you don't know enough to do so, meet with them and ask them to share their successes with you. You will likely discover they have strung together a long list of victories. The lesson to learn is that victories feed on themselves. A winning record feeds zest and creates positivity that fuels energy. Now, it is up to you to begin to create more wins.

SESSION 4

EXERCISE 1D – ZEST, ERODING

Session 4 focuses on ways you can begin to stop eroding by addressing insufficient zest. You must patch the leak before it makes sense to begin putting air back in the tire. There are four areas on which you should focus your attention.

Exercise 1 invites you to cultivate belief in your success. It is likely that you have become discouraged by the erosion of your life and are moving toward feeling a bit helpless to get your life back on course. Weakening belief in yourself and in your ability to create success will reduce your zest, making it more difficult to get yourself moving in the right direction.

TASK: Make a list of as many successes and victories you have created in your life as you can remember. Don't be concerned if they are big or small. It is likely that you are overlooking many times when you took on a challenge and won. Review this list every day for the next week and add to it. Notice how successful you have been at creating good things for yourself. This is the basis for your belief in your ability to do so now.

EXERCISE 2D – ZEST, ERODING

Exercise 2 invites you to focus your attention on things that are sucking your zest from you. If you pay attention, you may notice a variety of things that are undermining your zest. These might include people who are negative and who drain you of enthusiasm, joy, and hope. They might also include habits that lull you into apathetic acceptance of your circumstances. Spending hours watching television, for example, can undermine zest by diverting useful energy into wasting time. You may have other habits that leave you more discouraged and lethargic than energized and hopeful.

TASK: Make a list of as many zest sucks as possible. Determine to remove these from your life.

EXERCISE 3D – ZEST, ERODING

Exercise 3 invites you to focus on low-hanging fruit—interests you can pursue that immediately add to your zest. If you pay attention, you will discover you have numerous interests that actually make your life better and stronger. You may enjoy walking around the block in the evening but never connected it with feeding your zest and thus your energy to tackle issues that need to be addressed. You might have constructive and meaningful conversations with some people in your life that leave you feeling hopeful and energized.

TASK: Make a list of all of the things you are currently doing that actually feed your zest. When your list is complete, see if you can increase these. For example, you might determine to walk around the block every evening or to walk around two blocks. Feed those activities as much as you can until doing more would add no more zest.

EXERCISE 4D – ZEST, ERODING

Exercise 4 invites you to focus on activities you aren't currently doing that would increase your zest if you started doing them. You might not be doing any exercise and find walking around the block to be amazingly energizing. So, start walking around the block. You may discover an accounting class at the community college that is something you always wanted to do but never started. Take it and see if it adds to your zest. Finding and engaging in activities that feed zest is like following a trail of bread crumbs that lead to a more satisfying life.

TASK: Make a list of activities you believe would feed your zest. Start with the easiest one and begin doing it.

FACTOR – ZEST

Zest combined with enthusiasm, vigor, and vitality point to the energy you bring to life. Those who are high on this scale exude enthusiasm in all their pursuits. They are "gas pedals" for the world around them, advancing their plans and getting things done with vigor. Those who are low on this scale manifest a lethargy that is difficult for them to overcome. Everything seems as if it requires more energy than they have available.

SELF-ASSESSED RATING – TREADING WATER

You have sufficient energy, vitality, and vigor to maintain the life you have built but not enough to expand your life further.

SESSION 1
EXERCISE 1A – ZEST, TREADING WATER

You are treading water in your life because you have enough zest to avoid eroding but not enough to grow. Session 1 focuses you on different aspects of zest so you will better understand how they are currently operating in your life and how you can expand them. Let's get started.

Exercise 1 invites you to focus on your vitality. Vitality can be defined as your capacity for survival or for the continuation of a meaningful or purposeful existence. You might think of vitality as your expectation for your life. If you believe you should have a richer and more meaningful life, you will work harder to attain it. If, on the other hand, you have low vitality, you are likely to have low expectations and so are unwilling to exert much effort to make things better. Your vitality is sufficient to get you to the level of comfort and success you currently enjoy. You likely view yourself as someone who deserves moderate success, and your vitality is triggered when challenges threaten to undermine your situation, but you don't seem to have sufficient vitality to take on those opportunities and challenges necessary to grow.

TASK: List five opportunities or challenges you have been avoiding because you simply don't have enough vitality to take them on because you can't see yourself being that successful.

EXERCISE 2A – ZEST, TREADING WATER

Exercise 2 invites you to focus on your vigor. Vigor is your force of healthy growth. Think of vigor as that spark inside you that seeks to make your life better. It is almost an innate force that operates in all of us to press us to move forward. It was your vigor that motivated you to sit up, crawl, and walk as a child. Vigor pressed you to do your homework, to get good grades, and to better your life. Yet, it is clear that some people seem to have more vigor than others, and it is also true that life can, over time, add to or take away from our vigor. It requires vigor to achieve all that you have achieved in life. But, it takes more vigor than you currently possess to press forward for an even better life. Look back over the past 10 years.

TASK: Take some time to reflect and ask yourself if your vigor has increased or decreased. What is currently draining your vigor?

EXERCISE 3A – ZEST, TREADING WATER

Exercise 3 invites you to focus on your enthusiasm. Enthusiasm is absorbing or controlling possession of the mind by any interest or pursuit; lively interest. When you have high enthusiasm, your mind is active and engaged in the world around you. Whereas vitality is a way of thinking about your life and vigor is the natural force that seeks growth, enthusiasm describes the liveliness of your thoughts. You are full of enthusiasm when you are curious and open, scanning the world for new ideas, thoughts, and opportunities. Highly enthusiastic people are always reading new books, engaging in new hobbies, taking new courses, and meeting new friends. Enthusiasm opens you to new concepts and expands your view of the world. It seems that you have sufficient enthusiasm to maintain the life you have built for yourself. You aren't stagnating and regressing, but you don't seem to have enough enthusiasm to expand your life very much.

TASK: List five ways your life has expanded in the past five years. Has the expansion slowed or increased? Do you see yourself having increasing or decreasing enthusiasm?

EXERCISE 4A – ZEST, TREADING WATER

Exercise 4 invites you to focus on your energy, the final aspect of zest. Success in life requires significant energy. Every day brings its own challenges. Unless you are willing to exert yourself, you won't be able to maintain your current level of functioning. In order to move ahead and improve your life, you need not only enough energy to meet today's challenges but even more to advance and expand your life. Your life is pretty good. You don't need to make many changes, but if you want to get to the next level, you will need to take on some new activities, meet new people, try new things, and change your habits. It takes significant energy to do all that is required. You may not currently possess enough energy to make your life much better.

TASK: List five things you have thought about doing or contemplated changing that you haven't because you have lacked sufficient energy to do so.

SESSION 2
EXERCISE 1B – ZEST, TREADING WATER

Session 2 shifts your attention to some of the implications of having insufficient zest to move toward growing. Let's get started.

Exercise 1 invites you to appreciate all that zest has done for you to this point in your life. Now that you are familiar with the concept, you can see the role zest has played in your achievements. As you look back over your successes, you will see that your desire for more, your energy to move forward, your expectation of having a good life, and your naturally inquisitive mind pushed you to do things that were difficult and demanded a great deal of you but also substantially paid off .

TASK: Make a list of 10 of your accomplishments of which you are most proud. Notice the role zest played in each.

EXERCISE 2B – ZEST, TREADING WATER

Session 2 invites you to take a look around you. You may notice that there are many people you know whose lives are not nearly as successful and satisfying as yours. It is not an accident that this is the case. It is very likely that zest played a role.

TASK: Pick three people you know who haven't prospered as you have. Can you see ways they lacked sufficient zest to meet the challenges life sent their way? It is important for you to notice zest in your life and in the lives of others as a first step in nurturing and supporting greater zest.

EXERCISE 3B – ZEST, TREADING WATER

Exercise 3 invites you to take a look at those who are more successful than you. It is likely that you know people who have exceeded you in creating wealth, securing a better education, or building a better marriage or family life. Can you see the role that zest has played in their greater success?

TASK: Notice if they seemed to have greater energy in how they approached life than you have. Notice if they demonstrated more natural curiosity and a willingness to try new things. Notice if they had higher expectations for their life than you did. If it is true that zest is necessary for continued expansion of your life, you will need to learn to expand your zest.

EXERCISE 4B – ZEST, TREADING WATER

Exercise 4 invites you to consider how zest is trending in your life. There are only three options. First, your zest may be expanding. This is certainly the best pattern. Second, your zest might be holding steady—neither increasing nor decreasing. If that is true, you will need to do something to change the trend. Zest is like gas in the tank. You will need more for the journey to growing. Third, your zest may be decreasing. This is the worst-case scenario. Life can take its toll on you and, over time, wear you down to the point you begin to lose your zest for more. If this is true for you, you will need to stop the decline in your zest as quickly as possible. Treading water is not a bad place to be, but it is a hard place to maintain. It is likely that you are either getting ready to grow or you are getting ready to erode. It is up to you to decide the direction you want your life to go.

TASK: Reflect and ask yourself which trend you are on. Which do you decide you want for your life?

SESSION 3
EXERCISE 1C – ZEST, TREADING WATER

Session 3 focuses your attention on ways you can limit the reduction of zest in your life. You simply can't afford to have anything in your life that reduces your zest. Your zest is critical for your life to expand. Let's get started.

Exercise 1 invites you to consider your relationships with those close to you. You may notice that your friends and family members impact your zest in a variety of ways. First, they set an example for you by the degree of zest in their lives. If they have low zest, they make it easier for you to accept a lower level of your own. On the other hand, if they have high zest, they automatically encourage you to have more. Second, they can undermine your zest by discouraging you from taking on change and risk or they can encourage you to always be pressing for more and to be more engaged and energetic in your life.

TASK: List your five closest relationships. Which increase and which decrease your zest?

EXERCISE 2C – ZEST, TREADING WATER

Exercise 2 invites you to consider the habits you have formed. Habits are simply behaviors to which we grow accustomed and that become patterns. You may get used to watching television in the evening or having a cocktail after dinner. You may have a habit of completing a crossword puzzle every day or scanning the job board each week for new opportunities. Whether you realize it or not, your habits are either feeding or depleting your zest. Some habits may be lulling you into a contented sleep such that you have less interest and energy to seek your next challenge. Others may be creating interest in new things and feeding your desire to move forward.

TASK: Make a list of 10 habits you currently have. Which are adding to your zest and which are detracting from it?

EXERCISE 3C – ZEST, TREADING WATER

Exercise 3 invites you to consider your circumstances. Circumstances have to do with where you live, what you do for work, who you hang out with, which activities you participate in, and so on. Your circumstances can add to your energy and zest or reduce them. You may work with high-energy people who are always encouraging each other to learn new skills and cultivate new interests. Or, you might be in a job where there is nothing new to learn and all you do is repeat the same processes day after day. You might have a hobby, like travel, that takes you out of your comfort zone and exposes you to new cultures and ways of doing things. Or, you could have a hobby that you mastered long ago and now just maintain.

TASK: Make a list of circumstances that feed your zest and those that don't.

EXERCISE 4C – ZEST, TREADING WATER

Exercise 4 invites you to consider the last drain on zest: acceptance of the status quo. Let's face it, it is natural to come to accept things as they are, especially when they are pretty good. You might have a great deal of zest if you were facing some hardship or if your life wasn't living up to your expectations, but you have done pretty well for yourself and don't have a great deal of stress or problems to face. Acceptance of life as it is will reliably drain zest. You may have heard the story of the frog that jumped in a pot of cold water. The water temperature rose very slowly, only one degree at a time. The frog kept adjusting to the rise in water temperature until it got so hot, he boiled to death. Complacency destroys zest. Ambition, desire, hunger for more, curiosity, discontentment, and longing all feed it.

TASK: Take a good look at your life as you are currently living it. Do you find you are content? Do you see the impact of your acceptance of the status quo on your zest?

SESSION 4
EXERCISE 1D – ZEST, TREADING WATER

Session 4 focuses your attention on tools you can use to increase your zest and to apply it to growth. You have learned to identify zest in your life and to stop allowing it to decline. Now it is time to focus on how you can increase your zest. Let's get started.

Exercise 1 invites you to focus on something you want that you don't have. It really isn't that important what it is. You might want to lose 10 pounds so you can fit into that new bathing suit. Or you might want that new car you have been checking out online. It is important that whatever it is you want will require energy and effort to acquire.

TASK: Whatever you decided you want, write it down. Now, as you read it over again, notice your zest. Do you feel yourself energized to make that dream come true? Do you feel increased vitality? Setting any goal for yourself will build vitality. Pay attention to your zest. The more it grows, the more energy you will have to achieve your goals.

EXERCISE 2D – ZEST, TREADING WATER

Exercise 2 invites you to pay attention to whatever excites you. As was pointed out in the last exercise, having something you want can increase your zest, but so will anything that excites you. When you attend a concert and become part of a crowd of fans, you can feel your excitement rise. The excitement of the event will expand your zest. Being part of a team that is working together to do something interesting and important can be exciting and will feed your zest. Even watching a movie in which someone is being brave or taking a risk can vicariously feed your zest. The movie is calling you to be brave and take risks too. Pay attention to whatever excites you. It will lead you to those places where zest occurs naturally for you.

TASK: Make a list of five things that excite you. See if you can become more involved in at least one of them.

EXERCISE 3D – ZEST, TREADING WATER

Exercise 3 invites you to notice the things that get you in motion. It is difficult to build zest when you are by yourself and sitting still. The world is full of stimulation and interest. The more you are moving in the world, the more likely you will encounter events and people that stimulate your zest. You need to be busy and active. If you choose to play on a sports team, take up ice skating, visit a museum, or even take a walk, you are increasing the opportunity to expand your zest. Things in motion are easier to direct than those that are still. Your life is easier to direct when it is moving than when it is still.

TASK: Make a list of three things you could start doing that you aren't currently doing that would get and keep you in motion.

EXERCISE 4D – ZEST, TREADING WATER

Exercise 4 invites you to notice the things that are difficult to achieve. Zest rises to meet challenges, so the more difficult the challenge, the more zest is required to take it on. If you want to increase your zest, learn to challenge yourself with goals that take a great deal of effort to attain. You can choose to take a walk. It will take zest to get you out of your chair and onto the pavement. Signing up for a marathon will require zest of a whole greater order. Zest responds to challenge as muscles do to lifting weights. If your life weighs on you to the point that your muscles are exhausted, they repair themselves stronger. Zest increases to meet the challenges you take on and expands as a result of the success you achieve when they are completed.

TASK: Make a list of two difficult challenges you want to take on. Investing in these activities will expand your zest for the rest of your life.

FACTOR – ZEST

Zest combined with enthusiasm, vigor, and vitality point to the energy you bring to life. Those who are high on this scale exude enthusiasm in all their pursuits. They are "gas pedals" for the world around them, advancing their plans and getting things done with vigor. Those who are low on this scale manifest a lethargy that is difficult for them to overcome. Everything seems as if it requires more energy than they have available.

SELF-ASSESSED RATING – GROWING

You have sufficient energy, vitality, and vigor to expand your life but have some relationships or situations that sap your zest.

SESSION 1
EXERCISE 1A – ZEST, GROWING

You are growing because you have sufficient zest to keep improving and developing your life. You might think of zest as the energy and enjoyment that naturally propel your life forward. Zest is the fuel in your tank, the energy that drives change. But, even though you have been actively shaping your world, there is still more. You are not yet thriving. The goal of these exercises is to inform you about the nature of zest and ways you can more intentionally and thoughtfully apply zest to your growth. Let's get started by focusing on the four aspects of zest and what they might mean to you.

Exercise 1 invites you to focus on your vitality. Vitality can be defined as your capacity for survival or for the continuation of a meaningful or purposeful existence. You might think of vitality as your expectation for your life. Expectations are a key to releasing energy into your life. When expectations are low, you will tend to be accepting and lethargic. When expectations are high, you will be energized. Consider the current state of your expectations. Do you consciously feed your expectations by planning for future achievements, new adventures, and expanded experiences, or do you wait for life to bring them to you?

TASK: List five expectations you have for your future. If that is difficult, you may not be adequately cultivating your vitality.

EXERCISE 2A – ZEST, GROWING

Exercise 2 invites you to focus on your vigor. Vigor is your force of healthy growth. Think of vigor as that spark inside you that seeks to make your life better. It is almost an innate force that operates in all of us to press us to move forward. You certainly experience vigor or you would not have achieved all that you have. Vigor has stimulated you to always reach for more, to better your circumstances, to expand your experiences. Vigor is never satisfied. It is always growing and forever expanding. While your vigor has contributed greatly to your success in life, you may not have fully harnessed its full energy. There may have been times when you wanted to reach for more but were fearful or too lazy to actually move forward. You may have not always listened to your vigor and/or sided with it.

TASK: Review your last five years. When have you wanted more but not pursued it? What were your reasons? Were they valid?

EXERCISE 3A – ZEST, GROWING

Exercise 3 invites you to focus on your enthusiasm. Enthusiasm is absorbing or controlling possession of the mind by any interest or pursuit; lively interest. When you have high enthusiasm, your mind is active and engaged in the world around you. Whereas vitality is a way of thinking about your life and vigor is the natural force that seeks growth, enthusiasm describes the liveliness of your thoughts. You certainly experience enthusiasm for life. People who know you probably describe you to others as someone who is full of lively interest. You have interesting thoughts and lively conversations. You are likely known at work as someone who embraces your job with enthusiasm and is often coming up with novel and creative ideas. Your enthusiasm has contributed to the richness and success of your life, but there may be areas of your life where you experience less or no enthusiasm and so drain some of your zest from your life.

TASK: Review the major areas of your life: physical health and well-being, vocation, family, social, hobbies, rest, community, purpose. Note which ones are more filled with enthusiasm than others. Perhaps you have issues to resolve in one or two areas that, once addressed, will result in greater zest.

EXERCISE 4A – ZEST, GROWING

Exercise 4 invites you to focus on your energy, the final aspect of zest. Energy is what gets you out of bed and engaged in life. People who possess high energy are always on the go. It seems like they hardly ever sit still. They use time judiciously knowing that it is limited and precious. They prioritize their activities to make the best use of their time. People with high energy get a lot done. Clearly, you possess a great deal of energy—without it you could not have succeeded as you have. But there are two patterns that can undermine the optimal use of your energy. First, you could have a habit of pushing yourself too hard and then compensating by doing nothing or coasting. People in this pattern haven't yet discovered their ideal pace, the one they could sustain without crashing. Second, you could have some indulgences where you waste time and energy. This can be the result of bad habits or laziness.

TASK: Look at your life over the past three months. Do you see a pattern of being too energized followed by having too little energy? Or do you see activities or times when you choose to be de-energized and lazy? Why do you make those choices?

SESSION 2
EXERCISE 1B – ZEST, GROWING

Session 2 focuses on ways you can stop the loss of zest in your life. To the extent you are losing zest you are draining your life of the energy you need to thrive. You don't have many of these issues or you would not be as successful and satisfied as you are, but you aren't yet thriving and that suggests you may have some issues that need to be addressed. Let's get started.

Exercise 1 invites you to notice your thoughts in relation to your zest. Your thoughts can either encourage or discourage the zest in your life. Optimistic thoughts feed zest. When you believe you can do anything you want to do and have anything you want to have, your zest will expand. When you believe something is too hard for you or that you don't deserve something, your zest will be limited.

TASK: Consider your thoughts about things you might want to do or have. Do you notice any limitations in your thoughts? If so, identify those doubts or limits and begin to confront them by regularly imagining pushing past them. Do this until they disappear.

EXERCISE 2B – ZEST, GROWING

Exercise 2 invites you to notice your emotions. Emotions powerfully influence our zest. Sadness and depression can drain zest from your life as if your life is being pressed down and not allowed to be buoyant and vibrant. Joy and love operate in the opposite direction, contributing and adding to zest. It isn't likely that your life could be dominated by negative emotions such as sadness and anger or you would not have been able to achieve all that you have, but you may have times or some circumstances in your life where such negative feelings take hold of you.

TASK: Make a list of any places or circumstances where you experience sadness, anger, or fear. What can you do to shift from those feelings to happiness, excitement, and love? You need to work on this until you have eliminated the negative feelings from your experience.

EXERCISE 3B – ZEST, GROWING

Exercise 3 invites you to notice your sense of purpose and meaning. Purpose contributes to zest by providing a reason for being, a sense of bringing value beyond personal joy and satisfaction. Having a cause or noble purpose can be a great source of energy and vitality. On the other hand, the absence of a clear and compelling sense of purpose can limit zest. You may grow weary with bettering your own life at some point when further improvement makes only marginal increases in your happiness.

TASK: Write down the purpose of your life. If it isn't clear and/or compelling, you have work to do. Pursue a sense of meaning by asking yourself what is truly important to you and what difference you were meant to make in the world.

EXERCISE 4B – ZEST, GROWING

Exercise 4 invites you to focus on your relationships. People are social beings. Almost everything we do is connected in some way to another human being. You have many relationships—some close and others distant, some supportive and others contentious, some encouraging and, perhaps, others draining. Relationships can be a tremendous source of zest. You likely have many people in your life who love you, believe in you, encourage you, and support you. They are amazing assets. On the other hand, you may have some people in your life, even if only a few, who tend to be negative, critical, discouraging, and draining. People can drain your life by introducing drama that distracts you from your sense of peace. They can make demands on your time and resources that you won't want to give. They can leave you frustrated, irritated, and angry.

TASK: Make a list of relationships that feed your zest and a list of those that detract. What can you do with the relationships on the second list to mitigate their impact on your life? Work on this until you have solved each one.

SESSION 3
EXERCISE 1C – ZEST, GROWING

Session 3 focuses on ways you can increase your zest. Zest is critical for thriving. The more fuel you have for growth and expansion the easier it will be and the more quickly it will come. There are things you can do to encourage zest to grow in your life. Let's get started. Exercise 1 invites you to focus on being happy.

Happiness expands zest. So, the more you enjoy yourself, the more you have fun, the happier you are, the more zest you are likely to have. Happiness requires noticing what brings you joy and then choosing more of those things in your life. These choices can be big or small. Your friend might ask you where you want to go to dinner and immediately the new Italian restaurant comes to mind because they have the best lasagna you have ever tasted. But instead of saying you want to go there, you ask your friend where she wants to go and then head there. You didn't vote for your happiness. Asking for what you want doesn't mean you must always get it, but just stating what you want will feed your zest.

TASK: Make a list of five things you know make you happy. Determine to make those things happen sometime this week. Notice the impact on your zest.

EXERCISE 2C – ZEST, GROWING

Exercise 2 invites you to focus on your peace. When you are at peace, you are centered, quiet, open, and undisturbed. You might imagine that peace seems opposite of zest because peace does not always lead to action, but peace is like a battery that can store zest until the optimal time for its use. The opposite of peace is turmoil, tension, pressure, and activity for the sake of being active. Being at peace allows you to notice what is most important in your life. It allows you to dream dreams for your future. It allows you to clearly see what matters to you and what does not. It brings to light your opportunities and your obstacles. You can increase your zest by increasing your peacefulness. Review your daily schedule and note how often you are at peace.

TASK: Schedule into your day time to take a brief walk, a quick nap, some meditation, a conversation with a friend, reading a few pages of a book you enjoy, and listening to music. Small and regular opportunities to expand your peace will result in greater zest.

EXERCISE 3C – ZEST, GROWING

Exercise 3 invites you to focus on your love. Love feeds zest because it brings out your very best qualities. Love for others energizes you to become what is required for the best interest of the object of your love. Love gets you beyond the boundaries and limitations of your self-interest to the much bigger interest of the welfare of others. At the same time, resentment and hatred rob you of zest. If you are maintaining pain or resentment from some historic wound inflicted on you, you are putting yourself in the position of reduced zest. Your thoughts will turn inward and you will spend time attending to your festering wound.

TASK: Please make a list of any resentment, bitterness, or pain you have been holding on to. Release it. Next, write down five ways you can practice being more loving toward those in your world. Put them into practice.

EXERCISE 4C – ZEST, GROWING

Exercise 4 invites you to focus on meaning and how it impacts your zest. The more your life has a sense of purpose and meaning, the greater will be your zest. It is also the case that to the extent your life fails to have a clear and compelling sense of purpose you will experience a loss of zest. Purpose inspires engagement and action. Purpose seems to feed the human heart in ways that makes it stronger. Living your life only for yourself doesn't seem to be big enough to get the very best out of your life. If you want to expand your zest, consider enriching your meaning and purpose. You can do that by expanding your circle in many different ways. Volunteer at a shelter. Prepare meals for shut-ins. Visit people in the hospital. Take on a new friendship with someone who needs a friend.

TASK: Make a list of three ways you could add to the meaning and purpose of your life. Put at least one into action.

SESSION 4
EXERCISE 1D – ZEST, GROWING

Session 4 focuses your attention on ways you can apply your zest to your life that will take you from growing toward thriving.

Exercise 1 invites you to bring all of your zest into every one of your daily activities. It is likely that you have a great deal of energy from almost everything you do, but you may also discover that you have a few times during your day, or a few activities in which you regularly engage, where you don't seem to have much zest. In those times you are drifting, putting yourself on autopilot, and zoning out. Indulging in drifting is settling for less than the life you can have—one filled with zest in every moment and in every activity.

TASK: Take a few moments and list any times during your day or week when you drift. Write down next to each the reason you choose not to be more fully engaged during those times. Choose to either bring your zest to those moments or to replace them with activities filled with zest.

EXERCISE 2D – ZEST, GROWING

Exercise 2 invites you to bring your zest fully into your work and vocation. It is likely that you find a great deal of purpose and satisfaction in your work; otherwise you would not be growing. But you may not have brought all of your zest into your work. When you do, you will transform your work into a creative extension of yourself. Look for times or places at work where you aren't fully being yourself. Perhaps you aren't speaking up and expressing your thoughts fully, or you may be holding back some of your creativity by not asking to do the things you are best equipped to do. You may not need to make many tweaks to bring your work fully into alignment with your zest, but you would benefit from making every change that enhances your aliveness in your work.

TASK: Make a list of five changes you could make to bring more of your zest into your work. Put them into action.

EXERCISE 3D – ZEST, GROWING

Exercise 3 invites you to bring your zest fully into your relationships. You must have an abundance of healthy relationships in order to be growing, but relationships are one place where it is sometimes difficult to be fully alive because there are so many temptations to compromise our zest in order to maintain our connections to people in our life. Think through all of the people to whom you regularly relate and with whom you fully share your zest. You are fully yourself when you are with them. They delight in your honesty, openness, energy, and interests. They encourage you to be yourself and are themselves with you. Now, ask yourself if there are any relationships where you hold back to keep the peace or where you aren't yourself in order to accommodate someone who doesn't fully accept or appreciate you. These are the people with whom you are likely to sacrifice some of your zest in order to maintain the peace.

TASK: Consider how you can bring your zest into those relationships or how you will move away from those relationships in order to fully have your zest. This isn't easy but it is important.

EXERCISE 4D – ZEST, GROWING

Exercise 4 invites you to bring your zest fully into your meaning and purpose. We talked about the importance of having meaning and purpose in order to expand your zest in the previous session, but here we want you to consider how to shape your purpose by applying your zest. It is not enough to have purpose. We are challenging you to discover your unique purpose—the one that is perfectly designed to use all of your gifts, talents, and zest. It might be a journey to discover it, but it is a search worth making.

TASK: Begin by asking yourself what really matters to you and what difference you care most about making in the world. Then, get involved in that cause and see if your zest grows and expands. If so, keep following your enthusiasm and see where it takes you. Finding your unique purpose will fill your life with satisfaction and peace.

EXERCISE SERIES: ACCEPTANCE

FACTOR – ACCEPTANCE

Take information willingly, be open to new ideas and thoughts, and actively seek out this information to use for your betterment.

SELF-ASSESSED RATING – HANGING ON

You have almost no ability to accept the truth about you, your circumstances, and your life. Instead, you insist on believing things to be as you want them to be and resist feedback to the contrary.

SESSION 1

EXERCISE 1A – ACCEPTANCE, HANGING ON

You are hanging on by your fingernails largely because you have low acceptance in your life that is cutting you off from having true power. The purpose of these exercises is to assist you in understanding how you have gotten yourself in such a weak position so you can take responsibility for your choices and then begin to make better ones. Session 1 focuses your attention on the experience of being closed to feedback. You receive feedback from life many times every day. You get feedback from your bathroom scale, your friends and family, your doctor, your neighbor, and even your dog. The question is not "Am I getting feedback?" but "Am I open to listen to the feedback I am getting?" Since you are hanging on by your fingernails, it is more likely that you are closed, rather than open, to feedback. Let's get started.

Exercise 1 invites you to understand the concept of being conscious. Being conscious simply means being aware of what is going on around you. Everyone has filters and blinders that limit awareness to some degree.

TASK: Ask yourself the following very important question: How aware am I? Your answer to this question is very important because how you answer demonstrates your level of awareness. If you think you are fully aware, you are probably fooling yourself. If you know you aren't aware, you are on the right track.

EXERCISE 2A – ACCEPTANCE, HANGING ON

Exercise 2 explores the concept of unconsciousness. Unconsciousness is the extent to which we are not aware of all that is going on around us. People are unconscious to different degrees and over different issues. You are unconscious when you are holding on to attitudes, beliefs, and judgments against the feedback from the world that you are in error. You are unconscious when you choose not to think about issues that are bothersome to you as if by not thinking about them they stop being issues that need to be addressed. Unconsciousness is the effort to be blissfully ignorant. Can you see any evidence of being unconscious?

TASK: If so, write down those issues you might be choosing to ignore.

EXERCISE 3A – ACCEPTANCE, HANGING ON

Exercise 3 explores the idea of being militantly unconscious. When you are militantly unconscious, you are taking being unconscious to a whole new level. Here, you are fighting back against the feedback you are receiving as if you can change or nullify it. Not only are you in denial about the issues that are negatively impacting your life, you are actually attacking the source of the feedback in order to make it go away once and for all. Your problems don't go away, but at least you won't be hearing about them any longer. Militant unconsciousness is a problem, because whatever power you have available to make your life better is being used up in attacking the feedback that is pointing out your issues and problems.

TASK: To what extent do you see yourself as militantly unconscious? Over what issues are you militantly unconscious?

EXERCISE 4A – ACCEPTANCE, HANGING ON

Exercise 4 invites you to consider the decision to shut yourself off from the feedback you are receiving. It is likely that you don't consider this a decision at all. Instead, you view yourself as being attacked in some way by the feedback you are receiving and are simply trying to protect and defend yourself. You don't see feedback as information you need about issues in your life that need to be addressed. You get on the scale and when you don't like the weight that shows up, you throw the scale in the trash. You don't see that you made the choice of throwing out the scale instead of dealing with the issue it raised. The fundamental choice between listening to or avoiding feedback is fundamental to retaking control of your life. You can't continue to deal with feedback by choosing to ignore and put your life in better order. It is only when you are willing to choose to listen to feedback that you will have the information you need to get your life on a better course.

TASK: Can you see when you are choosing to shut yourself off from feedback? If so, list three illustrations.

SESSION 2
EXERCISE 1B – ACCEPTANCE, HANGING ON

Session 2 focuses your attention on the attitude of being defensive. This overlaps with being closed to feedback but adds the dimension of how you might shut yourself off from the feedback you are receiving. Others may see these behaviors as self-protective and self-serving while you may have come to see them as normal and reasonable. We hope to bring these maladaptive behaviors into focus for you so you can become aware of them and make different choices. Let's get started.

Exercise 1 invites you to notice when you make yourself content with issues that you know need to be addressed. We all do this to some extent. We grow accustomed to a level of messiness in the house and find it acceptable until company is coming over. Suddenly, our standard changes and we clean the house so our company doesn't see that we have been living with the mess. But when you accept too much messiness and disarray in your life, it begins to undermine the goodness and health of your life. Watching your career disintegrate over time, your health deteriorate, your weight get out of hand, your relationships become conflicted and contentious, and all manner of other problems without being alarmed and taking action is a problem.

TASK: Make a list of areas where you have made yourself content with issues that should be addressed.

EXERCISE 2B – ACCEPTANCE, HANGING ON

Exercise 2 invites you to see ways you excuse yourself for accepting the messiness and dysfunction in your life. There are many ways to excuse yourself from taking full responsibility for the difficulty and decay in your life. One of the most popular ways is to see yourself as not up to the task of managing your life. You may be telling yourself that you have special problems, weaknesses, or needs that let you off the hook. Perhaps you have health issues or you grew up in a difficult home. While such circumstances might make it more difficult to solve your problems and manage your life, they shouldn't be used as excuses. Excuses undermine your power by giving you an easy way out from doing the hard work that life requires.

TASK: Ask yourself where you are using excuses to avoid taking full responsibility for your life.

EXERCISE 3B – ACCEPTANCE, HANGING ON

Exercise 3 invites you to see ways you blame others to avoid taking responsibility for solving your own problems. Blaming others is not dissimilar from excusing yourself. Both are diversions from taking responsibility. It is easy to find people who aren't treating you as you expect or who aren't being fair in some way and to focus your complaints and energy on their misdeeds and wrongs. What you may not be seeing is that by paying attention to them you aren't paying attention to your life. Your situation continues to decline while you are railing on them. This is not a strategy that will improve your life. It will not add to your power. You are wasting your power where it will do no good.

TASK: Ask yourself whom you are blaming for your problems and situation.

EXERCISE 4B – ACCEPTANCE, HANGING ON

Exercise 4 invites you to consider all of the ways you justify being stuck where you are. You might be very creative in coming up with a list of reasons why you can't expect your life to be better than it is. Perhaps your family has the same problems, or you don't believe your life can be any better, or you know a lot of people who struggle with the same issues. None of that really matters. The only important question is this: Will you, starting today, take full responsibility both for the disarray in your life and for getting it in better shape? If the answer is no, your life will continue to decline until you are in serious trouble. If your answer is yes, you can begin harnessing your power to make positive change.

TASK: Answer the question: Will you start taking full responsibility for the disarray in your life and for getting it in better shape?

SESSION 3

EXERCISE 1C – ACCEPTANCE, HANGING ON

Session 3 focuses your attention on even more aggressive ways of avoiding responsibility for the state of your life by focusing all of your energy outward and chasing away whomever or whatever would shine a light on your lack of ownership of your state of affairs. This might be unpleasant for you, but it is important. Sometimes breakthroughs occur only when you come face to face with reality. Let's get started.

Exercise 1 invites you to focus on judgments you have toward others. A powerful way of downplaying feedback is to castigate the source. Finding or making up criticisms of those who demonstrate a more successful and powerful way of living may make you feel more accepting of your circumstances as they are. Notice the judgments you have toward the people in your world, especially those whose circumstances are better than yours.

TASK: Make a list. Can you see the self-serving nature of your judgments? Can you see how you use your judgments to deflect responsibility for your life?

EXERCISE 2C – ACCEPTANCE, HANGING ON

Exercise 2 invites you to see ways you might discount the feedback you receive from others because you don't think they understand your "special" circumstances. You hear what they are saying to you about your life, but you would prefer to think they don't understand you so their advice and counsel is of little or no value. You may have a well-rehearsed list of issues that you claim are unique to you and so beyond the ability of others to understand. You might say to yourself, *They have never been in my shoes. They have never had to struggle with my background. They have never had to deal with my health issues, family problems, emotional handicaps, or history of bad luck.* It might be true that the people who care about you have never been through what you have experienced, but that does not mean that their advice is not important and useful. Discounting feedback can simply be another way you are refusing to take responsibility for yourself and to make constructive changes.

TASK: List five times in the past month you have discounted feedback. Now, list what lessons you could learn from the feedback if you listened to it.

EXERCISE 3C – ACCEPTANCE, HANGING ON

Exercise 3 invites you to see ways you might be attacking the messenger to avoid hearing the message. You can "attack" the messenger in a variety of ways. You might not like the tone of voice your friend used when she shared the feedback. You might complain that you felt judged. You might get angry saying, "Whose business is it of yours to talk to me this way?" Or, you might become more openly attacking, slamming the door in your daughter's face or getting angry enough to get into a physical encounter. Anger and aggression are very useful ways of getting people to back off, shut up, and leave you alone. You couldn't send a more powerful signal that you are not interested in hearing what your friend has to say. You will have clearly communicated that it is dangerous to try to tell you what you need, but aren't open, to hear.

TASK: Make a list of times you have powered up and attacked people who in their care for you tried to deliver some message you didn't want to hear. Do you regret your behavior? Are you willing to apologize and ask them to repeat what they were trying to tell you?

EXERCISE 4C – ACCEPTANCE, HANGING ON

Exercise 4 invites you to focus on defaming those who seek to help you. Rather than showing appreciation for the goodwill your friends and family have toward you when they offer advice, you might make up stories about them, gossip about them behind their back, or spread rumors that put them in a negative light. This is your way of getting even. If they want to point out your shortcomings, you will make sure the world sees them in a similarly negative light. Rather than being defensive, you are on the attack. You have become vicious in punishing anyone who points out that area of your life you don't want to face. Your friends might be trying to tell you that you have a problem with alcohol or drugs that you aren't willing to face so you go after them and try to ruin their reputation. You may have actually caused reputational harm to people who care about you.

TASK: Make a list of people whom you have defamed. What can you do to repair the damage you have done?

SESSION 4
EXERCISE 1D – ACCEPTANCE, HANGING ON

Session 4 focuses your attention on the implications of cutting yourself off from the feedback you are receiving. You may not have any idea how much you are limiting yourself and actually creating the very problems that are undermining your life. Avoiding feedback is a bit like driving your car at night without the headlights on. You are moving forward but you can't see either the road or whatever obstacles that might be in your way. That is a dangerous way to drive. Not listening to feedback is a dangerous way to live. Let's get started.

Exercise 1 invites you to take ownership of the consequences of limiting your access to new information. You may have heard it said that the universe of what there is to know is divided between what you know, what you know you don't know, and what you don't know you don't know. That being the case, what you know is a very small slice of all that could be known. However, you are limiting what you know you are choosing to ignore aspects of reality. Choosing to address only a small subset of all there is to know makes it far more likely that you will make errors in judgment and poor decisions for your life.

TASK: List five places where your limited knowledge has created problems in your judgment and/or decisions.

EXERCISE 2D – ACCEPTANCE, HANGING ON

Exercise 2 invites you to see how cutting yourself off from feedback limits the challenges you need to take on to improve your life. Life is always challenging. Growth always takes seeing your limitations and putting out effort to change. You have been facing and overcoming challenges from the moment you were born. Taking on challenges is how you grow. When you limit feedback, you are choosing to ignore the very challenges you need to address. Your life won't get better until you turn to face them and to take them on.

TASK: List three challenges you are currently choosing to ignore rather than face.

EXERCISE 3D – ACCEPTANCE, HANGING ON

Exercise 3 invites you to see how cutting yourself off from feedback limits your opportunities. Life not only presents you with challenges but also with opportunities. You have gifts and abilities that the world needs and values. Feedback helps you to understand not only your weaknesses but also your strengths and where they can best be used in the world around you. When you limit feedback, it is like holing up in your house with the doors shut and the blinds pulled down. A lot might be happening in the world around you but you are unaware of all of it. Hence, you have no idea how to get involved. You have sidelined yourself. It is only as you get involved that your life can improve.

TASK: List five ways you have sidelined yourself and so limited your opportunities.

EXERCISE 4D – ACCEPTANCE, HANGING ON

Exercise 4 invites you to see how cutting yourself off from feedback limits change. Change is the one part of life you can count on. Tomorrow will be different from today. It is impossible to stop change and to hold life still. Unless you are changing, you are falling behind. To the extent you aren't listening to and learning from feedback you are failing to keep pace with the changing world around you. Of course it is challenging to see and accept the demands of your changing world. That is the challenge you must accept. To ignore it or deny it is to doom yourself to a steady slide toward irrelevance. This is the biggest risk of not inviting and accepting feedback. You become less useful and meaningful to the world around you. You simply can't let this happen to you. You can choose to change by choosing to listen to and learn from the feedback you receive.

TASK: Try it today.

FACTOR – ACCEPTANCE

Take information willingly, be open to new ideas and thoughts, and actively seek out this information to use for your betterment.

SELF-ASSESSED RATING – ERODING

You have some awareness but significant resistance to seeing things as they are, preferring to believe you are right and feedback is wrong.

SESSION 1

EXERCISE 1A – ACCEPTANCE, ERODING

You are eroding largely because you are only selectively open to feedback. Life is always giving you feedback. You get feedback from your bathroom scale, your friends and family, your doctor, your neighbors, and even your children. Feedback is necessary to accurately see what is working and what isn't working in your life. The question is not "Are you getting feedback?" but "Are you listening to the feedback you are receiving?" It isn't that you are shutting out all feedback. If you were, you would likely be hanging on by your fingernails. But you probably aren't listening to feedback in areas where your life is not going well. You have some serious issues that you are choosing to ignore and that are causing problems. Session 1 focuses your attention on ways you might be shutting out feedback and so cutting yourself off from the awareness that can lead to meaningful change.

Exercise 1 invites you to simply notice the difference between those areas where you are open to feedback and those where you aren't. You may not see that you have two categories for the feedback you are receiving. You may believe you are open to it all, but if you take a minute to think about it, you might begin to see that that is not the case.

TASK: Make two lists. On one write down feedback you welcome. On the other list feedback you resist.

EXERCISE 2A – ACCEPTANCE, ERODING

Exercise 2 invites you to consider the concept of denial and how it might apply to your openness to feedback. Denial is the unconscious or conscious choice to ignore some issue in your life. You may not want to admit you are overweight so you throw out your bathroom scale and buy bigger clothes. You may be drinking too much but tell yourself that everyone you know does the same thing. Denial gives you a way out of dealing with the issue. You choose to ignore the feedback you are receiving from the world around you. You might be able to see how dangerous denial can be. If you refuse to see an issue, you will do nothing to address it.

TASK: Make a list of any areas where you suspect you might be in denial.

EXERCISE 3A – ACCEPTANCE, ERODING

Exercise 3 invites you to notice where you are defensive. Defensiveness is often a sign of being in denial. You know you are defensive when you become irritated or angry when you are given feedback. You notice that you don't want to hear what others have to say or you start making excuses for things as they are. It is natural to become defensive. The important thing is to notice when you become defensive and to learn to shift to a posture of openness and learning. See if you can recognize when you become defensive and then wonder why you had that reaction. What were you avoiding?

TASK: Keep a journal this week and write down every time you become defensive. Write next to each instance the thing you were avoiding.

EXERCISE 4A – ACCEPTANCE, ERODING

Exercise 4 invites you to notice other manifestations of being closed to feedback. There are several. Explaining, justifying, complaining, criticizing, or blaming are different ways you can demonstrate your defensiveness. Each one diverts attention away from your behavior and either makes excuses or blames someone or something outside of yourself. Some of these behaviors may have become habits for you and so seem normal and acceptable. But, as you see them as ways you avoid facing feedback you need to accept, you can learn to ask yourself what you are trying to avoid. This is a tremendous and necessary step of growth if you are to shift from eroding to treading water.

TASK: Keep a journal this week and write down every time you catch yourself doing one of these five things: explaining, justifying, complaining, criticizing, or blaming. Then ask what you are seeking to avoid.

SESSION 2
EXERCISE 1B – ACCEPTANCE, ERODING

Session 2 focuses your attention on the consequences of not being open to feedback in some of the key areas in your life. It is important that you understand not only how you sidestep feedback but also the consequences of doing so. Let's get started.

Exercise 1 invites you to see clearly the impact of ignoring reality. Things don't change because you ignore them. At least they rarely change for the better. Problems and problem areas require your attention and effort if they are to improve. Turning a blind eye to your issues almost always results in continued decay and magnified problems. Most people don't seem to be willing to address their problems until they can no longer be avoided. It is only when fighting with your partner gets so out of hand that someone gets hurt that you realize what you are doing and how dangerous it is. It is only when you get caught stealing at work that you face the problem that has been going on for months. Closing yourself off from feedback is never the right choice. It is never helpful. It can only lead to less than optimal outcomes.

TASK: Ask yourself where you see yourself ignoring feedback. What are the potential consequences of continuing to do so?

EXERCISE 2B – ACCEPTANCE, ERODING

Exercise 2 invites you to consider the consequences of ignoring or underestimating your problems. Avoiding feedback is only one manifestation of ignoring your issues. Your life is your responsibility—all of it. It is of little value to take good care of your life in some areas if you allow problems to exist in other ones. You might take pride in eating well but overlook the outcome of having no control over your temper. It is your job to survey all of your life and to pay the closest attention to those areas that need the most work. This might not always be easy to do, but it is always the wisest course of action.

TASK: Make a list of the top three areas you should be taking care of that you currently are not.

EXERCISE 3B – ACCEPTANCE, ERODING

Exercise 3 invites you to notice how the things you have been avoiding have been going from bad to worse because you have been ignoring them. The garden that isn't tended to is soon overtaken by weeds. Your health condition that hasn't been addressed has likely been getting more chronic due to your inattention. Things don't usually remain unchanged. They are either getting better or getting worse.

TASK: List three issues you have been ignoring that have been getting worse. Track their deterioration and take responsibility for having already paid that price. Does this motivate you to change?

EXERCISE 4B – ACCEPTANCE, ERODING

Exercise 4 invites you to take responsibility for the fact that your unwillingness to accept feedback has cost you some relationships with people who genuinely care about you. The people who love you have been trying to help you for a long period of time by pointing out areas in your life that you need to address, but you have turned a deaf ear. On some occasions you may have become angry and hostile as if they were trying to harm you in some way. These well-meaning folks won't continue to try to get through to you forever. Eventually, they will grow weary and move on. They will write you off and stop trying to help.

TASK: Make a list of five people who have exited your life only because you have been unwilling to listen to and learn from them.

SESSION 3

EXERCISE 1C – ACCEPTANCE, ERODING

Session 3 focuses your attention on how others use feedback to strengthen their lives. Learning from others is a great way to see what does and doesn't work. You can then apply the things of value to your life. Let's get started.

Exercise 1 invites you to notice how open others are to accept and learn from feedback. It is likely that you have family and friends, some of whom are doing better and some of whom are doing worse than you are. Consider how they relate to feedback. Pay attention to how often they request feedback. Notice if they are open and curious or become defensive and angry. See if they seem to learn from feedback or fail to make any changes and persist in their old behavior.

TASK: Pick three people you know pretty well and whose lives are in better shape than yours and three whose lives are in worse shape. See if you can relate their success or lack thereof to their relationship to feedback. What can you learn from your observations?

EXERCISE 2C – ACCEPTANCE, ERODING

Exercise 2 invites you to notice how your friends and family try on the lessons they learn from feedback. It is never easy to hear tough things about ourselves. Who wants to hear that they are fat, or lazy, or harsh? It is so easy when you hear messages such as these to turn them away by discounting, denying, or explaining, yet you might notice that some of your more functional friends have a different approach. They may actually try on the feedback they receive to see if and how it might be true. In doing so, they demonstrate a radical commitment to improve their lives. Let's say you tell your best friend that she is lazy. She might quickly point out all of the things she does that show she isn't lazy. I am sure there are many examples. Or, she might look for ways she is lazy as if she is trying the feedback on to see if it fits in some way. She might discover that she frequently chills out on the couch in the evenings and is quite unproductive. This might be an example of laziness that, now that she sees it, she is ready to change.

TASK: Determine which of your friends "try on" feedback to see if it fits in some way.

EXERCISE 3C – ACCEPTANCE, ERODING

Exercise 3 invites you to notice how your friends and family generalize the feedback they receive. You may have received feedback that you drink too much and so now are limiting your consumption of alcohol and feel good about the progress you have made improving your life, but there is still more you can learn. You might ask yourself if, since you overindulge with alcohol, there are any other areas of your life where you might have that same tendency. When you ask yourself this question, you realize that you often overeat as well. Being open to feedback and generalizing it to other areas of your life can allow you to find new ways to change and grow.

TASK: Think of three people you know well and whose lives are in pretty good condition. Can you think of any ways they have benefited from generalizing the feedback they received from others? How could you benefit from doing the same thing?

EXERCISE 4C – ACCEPTANCE, ERODING

Exercise 4 invites you to notice how your friends and family make positive changes in response to feedback. Feedback is valuable only to the extent you do something with it. Feedback helps you see things you might not see or to appraise things differently than you may have been. Feedback points to ways your life is in disarray, habits that need to be changed, problems that need to be addressed. People who know how to use feedback wisely are always making changes based on the feedback they received. Their lives are always in a state of improvement and change. They are always giving up things and trying new things. One of the wonderful truths about life is that it keeps giving us feedback until we learn the lesson.

TASK: Notice if your friends who have very successful lives demonstrate a big appetite to make changes based on feedback. List some examples. How can you follow their example?

SESSION 4
EXERCISE 1D – ACCEPTANCE, ERODING

Session 4 focuses on specific skills related to feedback that you can put into place to arrest the eroding in your life. While none are complicated, they will require some new attitudes on your part. Let's get started.

Exercise 1 invites you to stop resisting feedback. Resistance to feedback ought to be easy for you to spot. Be on the lookout for things you don't want to talk about, issues you don't want people to address. Notice when you become defensive, deflect the conversation by changing the subject, or become irritated and angry. All of these are signs that you are resisting.

TASK: As soon as you notice resistance, stop, breathe, and remind yourself that there is something important to learn in whatever you are hearing. Quiet yourself and relax. Practice this every day for the next week.

EXERCISE 2D – ACCEPTANCE, ERODING

Exercise 2 invites you to learn to listen generously. Listening is not an easy skill to master. It seems we are far more inclined to want to be heard than to listen, but listening is far more valuable than talking because when you listen you are in the posture to learn. Listening generously means to listen without filters, to listen with curiosity and openness, to listen to learn and to grow. One of the ways you can practice listening generously is to repeat what you have heard. If you are doing a good job, you will not have embellished the feedback in any way. For example, your friend says you are lazy. You respond by saying, "What I hear you saying is that I am lazy. Is that right? You aren't arguing or resisting. You are simply listening.

TASK: Practice generous listening three times each day for the next week.

EXERCISE 3D – ACCEPTANCE, ERODING

Exercise 3 invites you to be honest with yourself. Your life is eroding. That is not good. It is not as if there is nothing you can do to stem the erosion. You are completely in control, but if you are going to improve your life, you need to know what you need to address. The only way you can know is to listen to the feedback from others. If you were going to an important business meeting, the last thing you might do is to look in a mirror. You want to make sure your appearance is sharp. The mirror neither likes you nor hates you, but it does reflect accurately how you look. Feedback gives you the information you need to strengthen your life, but you must be honest with yourself. You must be willing to admit your strengths and your weaknesses, your accomplishments and your failures, your good and bad habits.

TASK: Ask yourself where you might not be being honest with yourself now. Write down whatever comes to mind. Remember, your life depends on your honesty.

EXERCISE 4D – ACCEPTANCE, ERODING

Exercise 4 invites you to change. It is good to be open to feedback. It is helpful to listen generously. It is important to generalize so you can see how you can apply feedback to strengthen your situation. But not one of those skills does you any good until you actually change something. You don't have to change everything; you need to change only one thing. And the most important thing to change is the one change that will most arrest your erosion.

TASK: If you know what it is, make the change. If you don't know, ask some people who care about you and listen to their feedback. Then, change. You will be surprised by the power of making one change. You will show yourself that you are capable of taking control of your life and of making it better. That is a big deal.

FACTOR – ACCEPTANCE

Take information willingly, be open to new ideas and thoughts, and actively seek out this information to use for your betterment.

SELF-ASSESSED RATING – TREADING WATER

You are accepting of much of the feedback you get from the world, especially what affirms your strengths and accomplishments. You have some resistance to feedback that challenges you.

SESSION 1

EXERCISE 1A – ACCEPTANCE, TREADING WATER

You are treading water in your life largely because of your mixed relationship with feedback. In some areas of your life, you are open to feedback and learn from it, while in other areas you may be resisting or ignoring feedback that is necessary to your continuing growth. Session 1 focuses your attention on feedback skills you use but might not consciously understand. You are invited to pay closer attention to how you have used these skills and how they have contributed to your success.

Exercise 1 invites you to focus on the skill of generous listening. Listening is largely a lost art. So many people seem far more interested in talking than they are in listening, but listening is the key to constructive change. It is when you are listening that you are learning. Listening is important whether or not you like the message you are receiving. Listening doesn't filter out the parts that are easy to hear from the parts that are more difficult.

TASK: List five times when you have listened well to feedback in the past few months and how listening helped you to improve your life.

EXERCISE 2A – ACCEPTANCE, TREADING WATER

Session 1 invites you to focus on the skill of questioning. By questioning we don't mean doubting. Instead we mean asking questions to better understand exactly what the feedback means. Words can be taken many ways and can mean very different things. Questioning is the way you better understand the intent of feedback. Someone may tell you that you have a bad temper. You might consider a handful of questions to better understand: *When have you seen me lose my temper? What was I doing that led you to say I have a bad temper? With whom do I seem to have a bad temper?* All of these questions and others will help you gain a more complete understanding of the feedback you are receiving. Take some feedback you are currently receiving in your life.

TASK: Write five questions that could help you to better understand it.

EXERCISE 3A – ACCEPTANCE, TREADING WATER

Exercise 3 invites you to focus on the skill of claiming. One of the signs of defensiveness is discounting or denying feedback. When you are defensive, you are inclined to point out all of the ways it is not true, and, usually, there are many ways the feedback is not accurate. But the real value of feedback is experienced when you do the opposite—when you try it on for how it might be true. Claiming requires being open-minded and looking for examples of how the feedback is true about you. This is a radical step for many people.

TASK: Take the example from Exercise 2. You could point out many times when you have not lost your temper. There must be thousands of examples. But a more useful pursuit is to consider when you do lose your temper, with whom and why. Claiming feedback will open you up to new insights and expose you to areas of growth. Take one area of feedback you are currently receiving. Claim it. Write down five ways it might be true about you.

EXERCISE 4A – ACCEPTANCE, TREADING WATER

Exercise 4 invites you to focus on the skill of wondering. Wondering means you contemplate all of the ways this feedback can be useful to you. You take the time to "connect the dots" between the feedback you are receiving and how things have been working out in your life. You might consider if the fact you sometimes lose your temper cost you your last job or has gotten in the way of some friend-ships you have valued. Wondering expands the insights you have gained from feedback and opens you up to new applications of that knowledge.

TASK: Take one area of feedback you have received recently and "wonder" about how it can be applied to your life. Write down whatever insights come to mind.

SESSION 2
EXERCISE 1B – ACCEPTANCE, TREADING WATER

Session 2 focuses your attention on feedback skills that go beyond new thoughts and associations and are actually new behavior and changes that you have used to make your life better. Let's get started.

Exercise 1 invites you to consider how well you use the skill of appreciation. It takes courage to give you feedback, especially if it is about issues you might not want addressed. It is only those who genuinely care about you who will share with you the things you need to hear the most. You master appreciation when you take into account their love and concern for you and express it openly and directly to them. You might tell your sister that you appreciate her for telling you that you have a bad temper. That feedback has changed your life for the better. Not only is appreciation a way of thanking the people in your life for the care they show you, it also encourages them to continue to provide you with useful feedback.

TASK: List five people to whom you should have shown appreciation but have not. This week speak to each of them and thank them for the feedback they gave you.

EXERCISE 2B – ACCEPTANCE, TREADING WATER

Exercise 2 invites you to take on the skill of changing in response to feedback. The value of feedback is experienced only when you change in response to it. All the skills up to this one are wasted until you put feedback into action. The action required by the feedback you receive can be all kinds of things. You might give up a bad habit, get into therapy, try something new, take on a challenge, or make amends with someone with whom you have been holding a grudge. You see the signs of someone who has mastered receiving feedback by repeated changes that clean things up and make things better.

TASK: Make a list of five times you have received feedback and made changes in response to it. Now, list three areas where you are receiving feedback but have not yet changed. There is some work for you to do here.

EXERCISE 3B – ACCEPTANCE, TREADING WATER

Exercise 3 invites you to notice the relationship between your willingness to learn from feedback and your interaction with life as your teacher. There is no shortcut in living life effectively. There are things you must learn and challenges you must overcome if you are to grow and thrive. Life will bring to your attention the lesson you need to master at the right time. If you listen, learn, and change, you will have room to grow until it is time to master the next life lesson. If, on the other hand, you refuse to change, life will bring that same lesson to you over and over again, often increasing the cost of the learning until you are willing to pay attention.

TASK: Take a look at your life. Can you see that you have faced the same lesson on multiple occasions until you were willing to take it on? If so, what pain could you have saved yourself if you had only listened the first time? Write down the lessons you are currently facing.

EXERCISE 4B – ACCEPTANCE, TREADING WATER

Exercise 4 invites you to notice the relationship between your openness to feedback and the people in your life. The people who care about you are often telling you what they see about your life that would make things better. Not only do they point out problem areas, they also encourage you to see opportunities, abilities, and skills and how you could put them to use. Perhaps you have ignored some of their advice and persisted in patterns they know aren't best for you. You have also listened to them at times and have made changes that have improved the effectiveness and quality of your life. When they see you learn from the feedback they have given you, they are encouraged to continue to support and assist you. They are more likely to stay involved and to continue to coach you.

TASK: Make a list of the people who have been most helpful in coaching you by providing feedback to which you have listened. This is a good list for you to review frequently. You should make an effort to keep adding names. You can't have too many coaches.

SESSION 3

EXERCISE 1C – ACCEPTANCE, TREADING WATER

Session 3 invites you to see the consequences of not being fully open to feedback. There are times when and issues over which you resist feedback and refuse to make changes in your life. At times you can be stubborn or become defensive. It is very important that you recognize when you are entrenched and that you learn to shift to a learning posture at those times. Let's get started.

Exercise 1 invites you to consider the difference between the issues you tend to be open to addressing and those you tend to resist. If you look at the issues where you are open, you might realize they are the low-hanging fruit in your life—the easy issues. You might also realize that you have issues over which you might be insecure or embarrassed and so avoid. These are the hard issues. They make you feel uncomfortable when you think about them.

TASK: Make a list of easy and hard issues. Recognize that only if you are willing to tackle the hard issues will your life be what it could be.

EXERCISE 2C – ACCEPTANCE, TREADING WATER

Exercise 2 invites you to see your resistance to dealing with issues that would create problems for you. Growing can be messy. Sometimes it requires having some difficult conversations, making some big changes, altering some significant relationships. You might realize that some of the feedback you have been receiving requires you to make changes that will upset your life in some big ways. For that reason you have avoided the feedback and explained it away. It is time for you to realize that you are limiting the growth and effectiveness of your life by your unwillingness to avoid making a necessary mess.

TASK: Make a list of feedback you have been avoiding because you have been fearful of the consequences of making those changes. You have been avoiding upsetting someone or creating conflict. See if you are willing to move forward on these.

EXERCISE 3C – ACCEPTANCE, TREADING WATER

Exercise 3 invites you to notice your growth due to listening and learning from feedback. The fact that you are treading water means than you have learned enough life lessons to prevent your life from eroding. You are listening and changing, but it also suggests that you aren't listening to or learning from the feedback that would move you forward. It is highly likely that life is providing you with opportunities you are ignoring despite the fact that there are people in your life who are encouraging you to take them on. You are likely settling for less than you should have in life because you are comfortable.

TASK: Take a few moments and think about feedback you are currently receiving. Is there any you are ignoring? Are there any opportunities you aren't paying attention to? If so, list them. Next to each, write down why you are resisting and see if you are willing to shift to openness, curiosity, and making a change.

EXERCISE 4C – ACCEPTANCE, TREADING WATER

Exercise 4 invites you to notice where you might be avoiding feedback that is pushing you to face issues that are limiting your growth. Your life has a trajectory toward its maximum potential. Consider your height. You may be destined to be 5'10". You weren't born that tall but with proper nutrition you will grow to exactly that size. While you can't do much to make yourself taller, you can certainly do things that might result in now growing to 5'10". Your body naturally grows toward its potential, and unless you do something to prevent it, it will get there. Similarly, you are destined to a certain level of success, happiness, and love. You will naturally grow toward that level and will reach it unless you fail to cooperate fully with your life. You may have noticed this already in your life. You may be able to look back and see times when you messed up an opportunity or hung on to something that should have been surrendered long ago.

TASK: Make a list of those times when you failed to obey the lessons you were being taught and so interfered with the natural progression of your life.

SESSION 4
EXERCISE 1D – ACCEPTANCE, TREADING WATER

Session 4 focuses on specific ways you can apply your openness to feedback in order to move from treading water to thriving. Here you must be looking forward and thinking about making your life better. Let's get started.

Exercise 1 invites you to identify the one obstacle that is standing in the way of your growth at this very moment. It is always true that a journey is taken one step at a time. There is no reason to consider 10 steps from now when you are not willing to take the very next one. So, what is the one thing that is currently keeping you from growing?

TASK: If it is clear to you, write it down. If it is not, consider the feedback you are currently receiving. What have your friends been telling you about your next obstacle? What is your environment telling you? If you are open and paying attention, you should be able to become clear about your very next obstacle. Now you can decide if you are willing to take it on.

EXERCISE 2D – ACCEPTANCE, TREADING WATER

Exercise 2 invites you to consider what feedback is telling you about any habits that need to be jettisoned. Habits can undermine growth because they have become persistent behaviors that stop feeling like conscious choices and have come to feel like patterns from which we can't escape. You may have developed some habits that make you content with your current circumstances and so keep you from making your life better. You may consciously or unconsciously know that you can't move forward without giving up these comforting, but limiting, habits. You will know which habits need to change based on the feedback you are receiving about them. You might be getting feedback from your doctor that your cholesterol is too high, suggesting you need to cut back on the consumption of salt or need to get more exercise. Are you listening and changing, or are you ignoring and deflecting?

TASK: Make a list of habits you know you need to change. If nothing immediately comes to mind, review the feedback you are receiving and see if something comes to the surface.

EXERCISE 3D – ACCEPTANCE, TREADING WATER

Exercise 3 invites you to consider what feedback is telling you about the very next opportunity you need to take on. Opportunities are the only way to take the next step in your growth, but opportunities always require change. Change isn't easy for anyone. You must let go of the comfortable and take on something new and different. There is never certainty of success when you take on a new opportunity, but what is certain is that you must develop new skills if you are to succeed. It would appear you have been avoiding some opportunities in your life and have been receiving feedback to that effect for quite some time. You may know exactly what opportunity you need to step into or you may have grown so accustomed to ignoring it that you will need to review the feedback you have been getting in order to bring it into focus.

TASK: If you can, write it down. If not, consider what others have been encouraging you to do or what opportunities you have turned down. Are you now ready to step into it?

EXERCISE 4D – ACCEPTANCE, TREADING WATER

Exercise 4 invites you to consider life lessons you have been repeating and not mastering and what they tell you about what to do next. You might have discovered that you are a bit stuck, recycling through the same experience over and over or stumbling over the same problem without making a change. Such persistent problems tend to get worse every time you cycle through them as if they are amplifying the pain until they get your attention. If you are in such a pattern, your life is screaming at you to pay attention and to do something. This feedback is powerful and will continue to grow in power until you listen.

TASK: Write down whatever comes to mind as you read this. This challenge is something you need to resolve...NOW. Until you do, you will continue to repeat the problem but with more pain and suffering.

FACTOR – ACCEPTANCE

Take information willingly, be open to new ideas and thoughts, and actively seek out this information to use for your betterment.

SELF-ASSESSED RATING – GROWING

You are open to feedback about your strengths and weaknesses but may have one or two issues where you resist seeing and accepting the truth about yourself or your situation.

SESSION 1

EXERCISE 1A – ACCEPTANCE, GROWING

You are growing in your life. Congratulations! You probably recognize that your success is at least partly due to your relationship to feedback. You know you are constantly receiving feedback from a variety of sources and that all of the feedback you receive is useful in improving your life. You have done well learning from feedback and may be struggling to apply it to only a very few remaining issues. We want to start by reviewing the core aspects of openness to feedback so you are aware of their more subtle points. Session 1 reminds you of four of the most fundamental aspects of accepting feedback. Let's get started.

Exercise 1 asks you to focus on generous listening. Since the world is always giving you feedback, the most important question is "How well are you listening?" Not listening signals resistance to what you are hearing. Generous listening requires you to suspend judgment, to be completely non-defensive, and to hear everything that is being told to you without making any changes or filtering anything out.

TASK: You should be practicing generous listening in every conversation. You can test your skill at generous listening by repeating back what you are hearing. If you didn't repeat the entire message or changed it in some way, you should expect some resistance that needs to be identified. Give it a try this week and record any defensiveness you discover.

EXERCISE 2A – ACCEPTANCE, GROWING

Exercise 2 reminds you of the importance of asking clarifying questions in response to the feedback you are receiving. Good communication requires sending a clear message and hearing the message accurately. Accuracy and completeness are critical components to understanding. Since words can be taken to mean different things, asking good questions helps you better understand exactly what is intended in the feedback you are receiving. For example, your doctor might tell you that your blood pressure is high. You don't know if it is slightly elevated or seriously high unless you ask. You also don't know if the proper response is to take medication, begin an exercise program, or keep monitoring it. Good questions help you to understand precisely what is going on and the proper response for the feedback.

TASK: This week practice asking good questions. Notice when you aren't asking clarifying questions and wonder if it is because you are choosing not to understand more. This is a sign of being defensive.

EXERCISE 3A – ACCEPTANCE, GROWING

Exercise 3 reminds you of the power of claiming. Everyone becomes defensive from time to time. You might not always like hearing the truth, even if it is something you know you need to hear. When you are defensive, you will look for illustrations of how the feedback isn't true. You will point out all of the times you have kept a confidence and been trustworthy, of which there are likely many. But claiming moves in the opposite direction. You are claiming when you are seeking to find times when you betrayed a confidence and weren't trustworthy. There may not be as many of these occurrences, but it is by owning them that you will begin to understand why you behaved that way and how you can grow past such behavior.

TASK: Practice claiming this week. Take one piece of feedback you are receiving and look for ways it is true of you, even if it is difficult to do.

EXERCISE 4A – ACCEPTANCE, GROWING

Exercise 4 reminds you of the value of appreciating those who give you feedback. People who are willing to tell you the truth are exceptionally rare. Sometimes they tell you what you need, but don't want, to hear at great risk to the relationship. They have no idea if you will become angry, defensive, and write them off, or if you will be appreciative and grateful. Yet, despite the risk, they care enough about you to express their opinion about things you need to know. These folks are such valuable assets that you can't afford to lose a single one. Rather, you should not only value these people but seek to add to their ranks as many supporters as you can. One of the great tools in your toolbox to keep these people engaged is your willingness to openly and frequently express your appreciation for the feedback they give you. Not only can you thank them, you might also tell them what you learned about yourself as a result of their feedback, the changes you have made, and the impact it has had on your life.

TASK: Write down the name of three people to whom you could express such appreciation and practice with them this week.

SESSION 2

EXERCISE 1B – ACCEPTANCE, GROWING

Session 2 adds to your knowledge of the basic skills of being open to feedback and adds greater depth. You will explore ways you can become even more intentional in this critical skill. Let's get started.

Exercise 1 reminds you of the importance of actually making changes in response to the feedback you receive. Insight is a wonderful thing and self-knowledge is very important, but the real value of feedback isn't experienced unless and until you change in response to it. All feedback either points to something you are doing that is getting in your way or something you should start doing that will make your life better. The mark of a wise person is that she puts into use every lesson she learns.

TASK: Think through times when you have changed in response to feedback and times when you did not. It is likely that you will find examples of both. Hopefully, your list of times when have changed is longer than when you have not. Now, make a list of changes you know you should be making now. Are you ready to make them?

EXERCISE 2B – ACCEPTANCE, GROWING

Exercise 2 points you toward the value of intentionality. Perhaps much of the benefit you have received from feedback in the past has been pushed on you by circumstances. Things have gotten so bad and the feedback so loud that you could no longer ignore it. Life has a way of getting your attention even when you don't want it to. But if you choose to get intentional, you will respond more quickly to feedback and thus save yourself a great deal of aggravation and pain. You are intentional when you give thought to your life and when you seek feedback in areas where you think you might be missing something important. For example, suppose you keep being passed up for a promotion. You can either get angry about it or you can become intentional, asking your boss and coworkers what you might be doing or not doing that is getting in the way of your promotion. In this way you actively seek greater understanding.

TASK: Make a list of three places you could become more intentional in your life.

EXERCISE 3B – ACCEPTANCE, GROWING

Exercise 3 invites you to consider the value of reflection. Perhaps most of the time you are in action, actively shaping your world. There is certainly great value in getting things done and staying on the move, but there is also significant value in reflection—taking time out to survey the landscape and to assess all that is going on in your life. There might be great opportunities you are overlooking or some significant problems you have been missing because you haven't taken the time to regularly review the big picture of your life and to reflect on it. There is a proper schedule for reflection. You might set aside four hours on the first day of each month to review all aspects of your life and to ask yourself if there is anything that needs attention. You might set aside two hours on the first day of each week to think about what you want to accomplish that week and the challenges you face. You might start each day with 20 minutes of reflection to ensure you are focusing on the most important issues. Reflection can raise questions that feedback can address.

TASK: Decide on a schedule for reflection that fits your life and put it into practice.

EXERCISE 4B – ACCEPTANCE, GROWING

Exercise 4 invites you to properly consider the value of action. Just as reflection is necessary, action is as well. If you spend all of your time reflecting and seeking understanding but never take action, nothing will be different. Change requires action—sometimes action that is dangerous and risky. It isn't easy to complete a degree program or learn a new skill that prepares you for a new job in a different field. It isn't easy to break up with someone who will be angry and hurt, even when you know the relationship is not right for your life. You should value action and notice when you are backing away from action you need to take. Where do you find yourself to be fully engaged in change and where are you avoiding being in action?

TASK: Ask yourself if you are willing to take on those places you have been avoiding.

SESSION 3
EXERCISE 1C – ACCEPTANCE, GROWING

Session 3 shifts your attention to appreciating your success and the role openness to feedback has played in that success. Your life is in good condition because you listen, learn, and change. You are adaptable and flexible. Those are excellent qualities. We want you to appreciate how they have assisted you so you are encouraged to use them even more boldly. Let's get started.

Exercise 1 invites you to see how your openness to feedback has helped you to overcome obstacles that were in the path of your growth. Everyone faces obstacles from time to time. They are part of life. Sometimes they stop people from moving forward because they aren't able to find a creative way around them. When you met obstacles, you knew to first ask yourself, *What am I doing to create this obstacle? What do I have to do or what do I have to become in order to get past this?* By asking those questions you found ways to recreate yourself in new ways.

TASK: Make a list of five obstacles you overcame through the use of feedback.

EXERCISE 2C – ACCEPTANCE, GROWING

Exercise 2 invites you to see and value the connection between your openness to feedback and your ability to seize opportunity. Growth requires taking on new challenges, learning new things, and reconfiguring how we show up in the world. Opportunity always comes with risk. You must leave what is familiar to try what is unfamiliar. There is no certainty that you have what it takes to learn the new skill or gain the new knowledge necessary for success, but since you listened to feedback, you accepted the encouragement of others and their opinions about your capability and talent. Sometimes those comments were the very encouragement you needed to overcome your anxiety and to push forward. It is extremely valuable to notice the times you took a risk because you trusted the feedback you were getting from the people who care for you even more than you trusted your confidence in yourself.

TASK: Make a list of five times you took on a challenge or achieved something big because you listened to and learned from the feedback of others.

EXERCISE 3C – ACCEPTANCE, GROWING

Exercise 3 invites you to see and properly value the connection between the feedback you received and the change you have created in your life. It is no accident that you are growing even while many of your peers and friends are treading water or eroding. Perhaps you notice that some of your high school friends' lives haven't changed very much since graduation or that some of your college friends' lives are a mess. You have made significant changes in order to have a life in such good condition. You may have come to take those changes for granted and fail to notice how courageous you were and how many times you changed in the face of challenge or opportunity.

TASK: Make a list of five major changes you have made in your life. Next to each, write down the role feedback played. From where did you receive feedback? What did you learn about yourself? How did you change? How did the change benefit you?

EXERCISE 4C – ACCEPTANCE, GROWING

Exercise 4 invites you to survey your life in the broadest of terms and to appreciate your growth. This is such an important exercise because it gives you perspective of where you are on life's journey. You have certainly done a good job with your life, but you may not be finished yet. You have learned a lot from feedback, but there still might be more to learn.

TASK: Please write down all of the accomplishments of which you are proud. Notice the role feedback played in each. Now, consider your future. What do you imagine lies ahead? What accomplishments or changes do you imagine you will make? What do you think you will need to change about yourself in order to get there?

SESSION 4

EXERCISE 1D – ACCEPTANCE, GROWING

Session 4 focuses on the one or two issues you might be avoiding and how you can use the feedback you are receiving to move from growing to thriving. You can't be denying a great deal of feedback and be growing. Life just doesn't work that way. But you still aren't thriving, suggesting you may be ducking an issue or two that needs to be taken on and mastered. Let's get started.

Exercise 1 invites you to consider if you have some "sacred cow" you are unwilling to address regardless of the cost. You may have some issue rooted in your past that is currently standing in the way of your progress, but you won't deal with it because of some family values, past experiences, or misplaced loyalties. Some families have traditions they hold to be very precious, and you would be viewed as a rebel and outsider if you set them aside. You may have been through some tragedy or trauma that you would like to ignore but must face again if you are to grow beyond where you are currently. You are receiving feedback about this "sacred cow" even if you would like to ignore it. Face it now.

TASK: Write it down.

EXERCISE 2D – ACCEPTANCE, GROWING

Exercise 2 invites you to ask yourself if you have any frightening obstacles you are choosing to ignore. You have changed a lot in your life and have taken on many difficult challenges, but you might be up against one now that makes all of the others small. Perhaps you risked seeking promotions in the past and it was risky every time to take on a new role, but now you are contemplating changing fields and this step seems like too big a risk. Or perhaps you have done a lot of work on your marriage and confronted many obstacles, but now you know you are with the wrong person and the very idea of getting divorced stops you in your tracks. Sometimes life requires us to summon all of our courage and to take a very big risk not knowing how things will work out. It is in those times that feedback is most useful. Feedback may be telling you that it is the right decision to make even if you don't know where it will lead. Feedback might be reassuring you that you will be okay on the other side.

TASK: If you are facing such an obstacle, write down all of the feedback you are getting about this obstacle and how you should deal with it. Then summarize the big messages.

EXERCISE 3D – ACCEPTANCE, GROWING

Exercise 3 invites you to consider the big opportunity that you are facing and how that might change your life. Sometimes life will provide you with a new opportunity that may very well be a game changer for your life. You have finally met someone and are contemplating marriage. Now you are getting cold feet. You have always wanted to write a book. Now a publisher wants to publish it. You know if you move forward your life will never be the same again. Are you ready to give up the comfortable life you have for the unknown change you are creating? There is no necessity to take on this new opportunity. This is a place where feedback is extremely valuable. If you listen, you will hear a clear message either warning you that you are about to make a mistake or telling you that you are a fool not to move forward. While the message isn't always correct, it is always valuable input that you should consider fully.

TASK: If you are in such a situation, what is the feedback telling you to do?

EXERCISE 4D – ACCEPTANCE, GROWING

Exercise 4 invites you to consider the one fearful conflict that you have been avoiding even though you have been receiving feedback that it needs to be faced. While you may have been pretty fearless in speaking your mind and expressing your thoughts, you may have one person who refuses to acknowledge you for who you are and who persists in dominating you. It could be your boss who keeps taking credit for the work you do. Or it could be a parent who refuses to acknowledge that you are no longer a child. Regardless, you have been avoiding having that fierce conversation that is necessary if you are to continue to grow and move forward. Your irritation and frustration has been signaling that something is wrong and needs to be done but you have been trying to live with your negative feelings because you are too afraid to speak up.

TASK: Write down the one or two conflicts you have been avoiding. Now listen to your feelings about those situations and to the feedback you are receiving from others. Write it down. Are you ready to act?

EXERCISE SERIES: SELF-DISCIPLINE

FACTOR – SELF-DISCIPLINE

Able to stay focused on their goals and plans even when circumstances are difficult.

SELF-ASSESSED RATING – HANGING ON

You have almost no ability to discipline yourself in the service of reaching your own goals.

SESSION 1

EXERCISE 1A – SELF-DISCIPLINE, HANGING ON

You are hanging on by your fingernails in your life primarily because you have almost no self-discipline and so lack the ability to follow through on your goals and plans. As a result, you can't seem to get your act together and suffer at the mercy of whatever challenges life throws your way. Session 1 focuses on aspects of self-discipline so you are better able to understand the issues that are undermining your life. Let's get started.

Exercise 1 invites you to consider the importance of focus in creating a good life for yourself. Focus means that you are able to see all of the options available to you and all of the noise going on in your life and can narrow things down to the one or two issues that most need your attention. Focus is the beginning of self-discipline. Without focus you have no idea what to discipline yourself to do. You will know you lack focus if you are scattered, overwhelmed, and see your life as having too many things going on to have any idea what is most important.

TASK: Write down any evidence of focus you see in your life.

EXERCISE 2A – SELF-DISCIPLINE, HANGING ON

Exercise 2 invites you to consider the role of delayed gratification in self-discipline. Everyone would like to have what they want when they want it, but you may have come to see that sometimes you must put off what you want now in order to create something better later. You may prefer playing with your friends instead of doing your homework, but if you don't do your homework, you won't set yourself up for success in your education. Your career and life will suffer. You must learn to put off what you want in the moment to do what is more important. It is likely that you are not very good at delaying gratification. You may be in the habit of giving in to whatever whim or wish you have.

TASK: Write down five instances where you have demonstrated the ability to delay gratification.

EXERCISE 3A – SELF-DISCIPLINE, HANGING ON

Exercise 3 invites you to consider the importance of the ability to say no to yourself. While similar to delaying gratification, sometimes it is necessary to say no to something that is counterproductive and harmful. It might be pleasurable, but it is destructive. You may have encountered such instances around issues like eating sweets, drinking alcohol, taking drugs, or having sex. None of those things is necessarily harmful or bad, but unless you have the ability to say no to yourself, every one of them can undermine your life in serious ways. Part of maturing as a person is learning the ability to turn away from things that will do us harm.

TASK: List three things you have wanted and to which you have said no to yourself.

EXERCISE 4A – SELF-DISCIPLINE, HANGING ON

Exercise 4 invites you to make the connection between distractibility and the self-discipline you need for a productive life. You may have had times in your life where you had a clear and positive goal that you were excited to achieve and set out to make it happen, only to find that something else quickly caught your attention and distracted you from your goal. There are always many interesting and exciting things to do in life that compete for your attention. Unless you can avoid being distracted and can stay focused on the goals you have set for yourself, you will find yourself in a pattern of having started many things and having completed none of them. You simply must learn how to keep yourself from becoming distracted.

TASK: List five times you can remember being tempted to be distracted but successfully stayed your course.

SESSION 2
EXERCISE 1B – SELF-DISCIPLINE, HANGING ON

Session 2 continues to focus you on aspects of self-discipline that you need to understand in order to gain control of your life. It is important that you notice where you lack self-discipline so you can strengthen yourself in those areas. Let's get started.

Exercise 1 invites you to see the importance of sustained focus on whatever goals you believe to be important. This is the skill that helps you avoid being distracted. You are able to sustain your focus to the extent you can keep your goals in mind and maintain excitement about the benefit their achievement will bring to your life. Sustaining focus requires you to envision your future and to believe you can create good things for yourself. To the extent you see your life as out of your control or you lose faith that you can manage it, you will have difficulty sustaining focus on your goals.

TASK: To what extent do you have the ability to sustain focus on your goals from 1 (high) to 5 (low)?

EXERCISE 2B – SELF-DISCIPLINE, HANGING ON

Exercise 2 invites you to consider the role of courage in self-discipline. It would be nice if you never encountered any obstacles or problems, but that is hardly ever the case. Self-discipline is tested when you face difficulties. Will you stay on course despite the challenges you are facing? Or will you become discouraged and give up? Courage pushes you to persist through difficulties and to stay on course even when things are hard. Notice how you have managed challenges and difficulties in your life. Did you have the courage to persevere or did you quit?

TASK: Make a list of times when you demonstrated courage and times when you didn't.

EXERCISE 3B – SELF-DISCIPLINE, HANGING ON

Exercise 3 invites you to consider your tolerance for pain. Sometimes the pathway to your goal will require some sort of suffering. Not only may you encounter difficulties, but things can become quite unpleasant and even painful. For example, if you set a goal of running a marathon, you might really enjoy warming up, being part of the crowd, the energy at the starting line, and that initial jump off the line. But when you are into the race and getting near the 20-mile marker, you are likely to notice pain. Your legs hurt, you are winded, and you are running out of energy. Only if you are able to tolerate pain will you be able to finish the race. Otherwise, as soon as you become uncomfortable, you will quit. The ability to tolerate pain is critical to self-discipline.

TASK: How good are you at tolerating discomfort and pain from 1 (very good) to 5 (not good at all)?

EXERCISE 4B – SELF-DISCIPLINE, HANGING ON

Exercise 4 invites you to consider the role of perseverance in self-discipline. You establish habits and patterns in how you deal with goals and difficulties. If you start many things that you later quit because you were distracted or they became too difficult for you, you are creating the habit of quitting. You are teaching yourself to give up when things reach a certain level of discomfort. On the other hand, if you finish what you start, you are creating the habit of perseverance. You are teaching yourself how to stick with and drive through to completion whatever you choose to take on. The habit of perseverance can be extremely helpful when you are facing challenges and are tempted to quit. It is likely that you have not done an especially good job at cultivating perseverance and will need to build this habit from the ground up. The best way to do so is to start with small and easy goals and then to build confidence through your track record of finishing what you start.

TASK: List five goals where you finished what you started.

SESSION 3
EXERCISE 1C – SELF-DISCIPLINE, HANGING ON

Session 3 focuses on the consequences of having little or no self-discipline on the quality of your life. It is important that you understand the price you are paying for not cultivating greater self-discipline. Let's get started.

Exercise 1 invites you to consider the cost of having no clarity about how you want your life to be. Without self-discipline there is little value in having a vision or goal for your life as you lack the capacity to create that vision or reach that goal. Hence, you have likely accepted your circumstances with no sense that you can improve them in any way. Without a clear goal, it is unlikely that things will get much better.

TASK: Write down your vision for your life. You may struggle to know what to write. Or, you may write something so vague and grandiose that it is of little value in guiding your behavior.

EXERCISE 2C – SELF-DISCIPLINE, HANGING ON

Exercise 2 invites you to see if you have a clear plan for how you will make your life better. Since you have little self-discipline, it is likely that you have started many times to make changes in your life but either became distracted or gave up when you encountered problems or obstacles. Hence, your track record for improving your life is not good. Even if you had a vision or goal, you would not know how to begin or progress toward that goal. What good is a plan if you don't follow it? Since you have not followed plans you have made in the past, you likely don't see much value in creating plans now. Without a plan, change will seem overwhelming and impossible.

TASK: If this is how you are feeling, note how often you create plans for change.

EXERCISE 3C – SELF-DISCIPLINE, HANGING ON

Exercise 3 invites you to consider how often you stick with your plans and actually see them through to completion. You probably have a long list of projects you have started but not completed, of changes you wanted to make but never quite accomplished. This is the key evidence of poor self-discipline. The pattern of not following through will undermine your self-confidence as well as the confidence of others that you will benefit from their encouragement and assistance. You will gradually come to the conclusion that change is hopeless for you because you can't stay focused and on track for much of anything.

TASK: Make a list of changes or projects you have started but not completed.

EXERCISE 4C – SELF-DISCIPLINE, HANGING ON

Exercise 4 invites you to consider the sense of defeat, helplessness, and hopelessness that result from poor self-discipline. Eventually, you will give up on yourself. You will come to the conclusion that your life is completely out of your control. You might not know what to do to make things better, but even if you did, you lack the ability to implement any constructive change. The attitude of defeat is serious because it will undermine any hope that things can be better. It is a place of giving up. It is our hope that you won't allow yourself to reach the place of defeat but will take whatever strength and conviction you have remaining to change course and to begin making your life stronger.

TASK: Rate your sense of being defeated from 1 (hopeless) to 5 (you know you can turn things around).

SESSION 4

EXERCISE 1D – SELF-DISCIPLINE, HANGING ON

Session 4 focuses on some basic steps you can take to begin to arrest the decline in your life by laying the foundation for self-discipline. These are basic steps but are critically important. Let's get started.

Exercise 1 invites you to make the success and goodness of your life really important to you. It must become more important than doing what is easy, having fun, and being lazy. And, if this is too big an idea for you to get behind, it is okay to focus on just one thing you want for your life that would make it better and that you will make extremely important.

TASK: If you can think of one thing, write it down. Next, write how your life will be better when you succeed in this achievement. Put this on your refrigerator or someplace you will review it every day as a way to keep your enthusiasm high.

EXERCISE 2D – SELF-DISCIPLINE, HANGING ON

Exercise 2 invites you to create a reasonable plan for how you will accomplish the goal you wrote down in Exercise 1. It is too much to ask of yourself to sign up for a goal without knowing the plan of how you will achieve it. For example, if you chose to lose 20 pounds, it would be so easy to become discouraged. If you decide you will start by counting your calories each day, it will be much easier to stick with it. Your plan should start with the most basic first step and then the next and the next until you have achieved your goal.

TASK: Write out your plan and show it to someone who cares about you. Ask for their feedback as to whether your plan is complete and properly challenging.

EXERCISE 3D – SELF-DISCIPLINE, HANGING ON

Exercise 3 invites you to strengthen your belief that you can succeed. Belief is everything. Until you can believe in yourself and your ability to shape your life in a positive manner, it will be very difficult for you to cultivate your self-discipline. Look around you at people you know whose lives are in much better shape than yours. Can you see that they aren't necessarily smarter, more talented, or more experienced than you are? One thing they might have going for them is that they believe they can get almost everything they are willing to work for. They don't think it will necessarily come easy, but they believe that if they stick with it, work hard, and are willing to go through some suffering and pain, they can get to their goal. This is a critical lesson for you to learn.

TASK: You can start by listing five times in your life when you have created something good for your life. You might have attracted an amazing partner, completed your education, landed a decent job, and bought a house. Every accomplishment required you to show up, do all that was required, and get to the goal. You need to keep reminding yourself that you can do anything you set your mind to.

EXERCISE 4D – SELF-DISCIPLINE, HANGING ON

Exercise 4 invites you to take action. You can read these exercises and make lists, but until you sign up to change something and experience success, you won't have significantly expanded your self-discipline. Self-discipline grows only through the experience of setting a goal, sticking with it, overcoming obstacles, avoiding distractions, being courageous, and getting to where you set out to go. And, the more often you successfully repeat that process, the more your self-discipline will grow. You will learn how to keep yourself focused, encourage yourself to keep going, and avoid distractions, so take one small thing you want to improve or achieve. Be very specific.

TASK: Write a plan that starts with the very first step and includes all of the steps to reach the goal. Share your plan with your support network and ask for their help in staying focused. Now, take step one.

FACTOR – SELF-DISCIPLINE

Able to stay focused on their goals and plans even when circumstances are difficult.

SELF-ASSESSED RATING – ERODING

You have insufficient ability to discipline yourself to accomplish many of your goals.

SESSION 1

EXERCISE 1A – SELF-DISCIPLINE, ERODING

Your life is eroding primarily because your poor self-discipline makes it very difficult for you to stick with the plans you make to improve your circumstances. The goal of these exercises is to help you to better understand the components of self-discipline and to see how they impact your life both positively and negatively. Session 1 points out some of the key elements of self-discipline.

Exercise 1 invites you to consider the role clear goals play in self-discipline. As long as your goals are absent or poorly defined, there is nothing requiring discipline. You are free to go wherever the winds of circumstance take you. Unfortunately, such a style of living is rarely effective and almost always leads to unresolved problems, declining success, and chaos.

TASK: List five goals you currently have for your life. As you review them, note if they are clear and specific.

EXERCISE 2A – SELF-DISCIPLINE, ERODING

Exercise 2 invites you to consider if you have too many or conflicting goals. It is one thing to have no goals or to have goals that aren't clear. It is a different problem to have so many goals that there is no priority or to have goals that conflict with each other. You could have a goal to save money and a goal to do some substantial home improvements. It is not clear how you could do both at the same time. Conflicting goals cancel each other out and tend to lead to confusion and inaction. You could unconsciously be creating the illusion of order when, in fact, you are giving yourself an excuse to be undisciplined. Conflicting goals allow you to complain you have so many things to do, you can't really do anything.

TASK: List any conflicting goals you might have. Note also if you have so many goals that you are overwhelmed by them.

EXERCISE 3A – SELF-DISCIPLINE, ERODING

Exercise 3 invites you to consider if you have sufficiently well-conceived plans. You may have very clear and appropriate goals but never create plans that are actionable. Without actionable plans, it is extremely difficult, if not impossible, to discipline yourself to staying on course. Plans organize your thoughts and focus your energy. They provide a pace for change that is reasonable. Without a complete plan, you can easily wander to whatever catches your attention, so ask yourself if you are skilled at creating plans for the important goals in your life.

TASK: If you think you are, list three examples of plans you are currently using. When you write them down, review them to see how reasonable they are. If not, consider why you haven't created plans. Perhaps you did not know they were important.

EXERCISE 4A – SELF-DISCIPLINE, ERODING

Exercise 4 invites you to consider the possibility that while you have plans, they are either too complex or too many to be useful in disciplining yourself to stay on course. A good plan is like a roadmap; it provides clear guidance as to the route you will take to get from one place to another. Once you decide on the route, your only task is to follow it. You don't need to make many choices as to which turn to take. But, if you have competing plans or conflicting plans, you will only make it harder to stick with your journey. You will introduce the need to make decisions that slow you down and create confusion.

TASK: Write down one plan you have to make any change in your life. Is it simple and easy to follow? Or it is overly complex and difficult? If it is complex, try simplifying it.

SESSION 2
EXERCISE 1B – SELF-DISCIPLINE, ERODING

Session 2 focuses on a variety of ways poor self-discipline can show up in your life and can undermine your success. The goal of these exercises is to assist you in seeing patterns of behavior with which you may have become familiar and accustomed but need to be viewed as problematic. Let's get started.

Exercise 1 invites you to recognize insufficient ability to say no to yourself. Learning to say no to yourself is a critical skill in maturing. Every day many interesting things will catch your eye and will invite your attention. Unless you can choose between them and say no to most of them, it will be impossible to move forward in any meaningful way. Perhaps you have seen parents with very young children who get stuck at the candy display at the grocery store. The children seem to want every candy available, and the poor parent is just trying to get out of the store. Encouragement to make up your mind seems to fall on deaf ears.

TASK: Rate your ability to say no to yourself from 1 (no problem at all) to 5 (extremely difficult). List five things about which you know you should say no to yourself.

EXERCISE 2B – SELF-DISCIPLINE, ERODING

Exercise 2 invites you to notice if you have difficulty sticking to a plan—any plan. Following a plan takes self-discipline. All of the steps are laid out, but, in order for the goal to be reached, the plan must be carefully followed. Some people have unresolved authority issues and don't like to be told what to do. A plan feels too much like someone is dictating your choices and you rebel against it. For others, a plan seems too limiting. You may want the freedom to decide to do whatever you feel like doing in every moment regardless of the plan. However, unless you can follow plans, you will have difficulty preventing your life from eroding.

TASK: Rate your ability to follow a plan from 1 (excellent) to 5 (impossible). List three plans you should be following because you know they would be good for you.

EXERCISE 3B – SELF-DISCIPLINE, ERODING

Exercise 3 invites you to notice if you have trouble dealing with difficulty. Rarely does growth come without challenge, conflict, problems, and resistance. You may not have trouble following your plans until you encounter difficulty. At that point, you quit. You just don't seem to have the courage to overcome the obstacles in your path. You can't discipline yourself to stick with your goals when times get tough and you face opposition. Opposition can come from many places. Sometimes it is internal and shows up as self-talk that convinces you that you aren't capable of succeeding. Sometimes opposition comes from the people in your life who may be threatened by the changes you want to make. At other times, opposition is just the challenges of doing new things.

TASK: Rate your ability to discipline yourself when you face challenges from 1 (excellent) to 5 (very poor). List three obstacles you are now facing.

EXERCISE 4B – SELF-DISCIPLINE, ERODING

Exercise 4 invites you to notice how easy it is for you to simply give up. You may be one of those people who seem to give up on things a lot. You might give up on your dreams because they seem to be too good for you. Or, you might give up on your plans when you hit trouble. Or, you might give up on any hope that your life could be better. Self-discipline requires the ability to persevere regardless of circumstances and difficulties. There is great value in being able to keep putting one foot in front of the other no matter how difficult the journey. Giving up can become a habit that is difficult to break.

TASK: Rate your ability to discipline yourself to keep moving forward and not give up from 1 (excellent) to 5 (very poor). List three times you were tempted to but didn't give up on something that mattered to you.

SESSION 3
EXERCISE 1C – SELF-DISCIPLINE, ERODING

Session 3 focuses your attention on the impact of your poor self-discipline on the quality of your life. It is no accident that your life is eroding. Self-discipline is a critical component of a successful life. Let's examine some of the implications of lacking adequate self-discipline. Exercise 1 invites you to focus on your grave-yard of goals. You may be quite good at having good ideas about what you want for your life but aren't nearly as skilled at following through. The result is that you have a "graveyard" filled with your dreams, goals, and visions that died before they came to life. You keep telling yourself it will be different this time as you set off on a new weight loss plan or tell your friends you are going to change jobs, but because you can't seem to hold your course, something always happens that sidetracks your plans and leaves your life unchanged. You may not even be aware of how many goals you have had that have led nowhere.

TASK: Make a list of as many as you can recall. Do you see a pattern of thinking big but accomplishing very little?

EXERCISE 2C – SELF-DISCIPLINE, ERODING

Exercise 2 invites you to notice the impact of your poor self-discipline on your self-esteem. Self-esteem simply means how you judge or value yourself. While you might not want to admit it, your inability to follow through on your goals and plans undermines your sense of confidence and competence. You know you lack the ability to say no to yourself and to keep yourself from wandering toward whatever catches your attention. You see that you have a graveyard full of promises you have made to yourself that have never come true. You have come to not trust your own ability to do what is necessary to care for your own life. Your low self-confidence now undermines your ability to try new things or to take on much, if any, change. In order to help you come to grips with the impact of your poor self-discipline on your self-esteem, we invite you to write down what you think about yourself. How much confidence do you have in your ability to follow through on things that you know are good for you?

TASK: Rate your confidence from 1 (very high) to 5 (very low). Make a list of five of your dreams that you didn't bring to life.

EXERCISE 3C – SELF-DISCIPLINE, ERODING

Exercise 3 invites you to notice and take responsibility for the impact your poor self-discipline has on the people in your life who care about you and believe in you. The people who love you have watched you struggle. They want better things for you, and when you announce your plans to change, they not only encourage you but also offer assistance. Then, when you fail to follow through, they begin to lose faith in you and to see you as someone who will never succeed. Your inability to discipline yourself is using up their goodwill. Over time, they will begin to distance themselves from you and will invest their energy and assistance in those who are better able to put it to good use.

TASK: Make a list of people who have given up on you as a result of your poor self-discipline.

EXERCISE 4C – SELF-DISCIPLINE, ERODING

Exercise 4 invites you to notice and take responsibility for the pattern of failure that leads to discouragement and, eventually, to hopelessness. Your lack of self-discipline has cost you a great deal. You may have noticed the individual dreams that were not brought to life and some of the plans you created but failed to execute. What you may not clearly see is the pattern you have established and the implications of that pattern for your future. Your lack of execution is undermining your confidence that you can complete anything of value. The more you come to believe that to be true, the less able you will be to take on any challenge and to make any improvement. At some point, you could give up on yourself completely. It is so important that you not allow that to happen. You must establish a pattern of following through.

TASK: Make a list of some things, even if they are small, that you have completed.

SESSION 4
EXERCISE 1D – SELF-DISCIPLINE, ERODING

Session 4 focuses your attention on some fundamental steps to begin building better self-discipline. While these lessons might seem simple to understand, they are not always easy to master. Let's get started. Exercise 1 invites you to pick something small to take on. One of the big mistakes in building self-discipline is to take on a big and complex goal that will take a long time to achieve. It is so big and so distant that it is difficult to see progress along the way, so it is easy to become discouraged and/or distracted. Instead, pick something you want to change or achieve that will make your life better. The smaller the better. For example, if your big goal is to eat healthy food, make your smaller goal something like learning which foods are healthy. This is a critical step toward the bigger goal and it is something that won't take more than 20-30 minutes to achieve.

TASK: Take some time now to pick your one thing. Write it down.

EXERCISE 2D – SELF-DISCIPLINE, ERODING

Exercise 2 invites you to focus only on today. When you focus on where you want to be a year from now, you might become overwhelmed by all of the changes you will need to make to get there. If you overwhelm yourself, it will be more difficult to discipline yourself to stay on course. Instead, focus only on today. What are you going to do today to move toward your goal? If we use the example from Exercise 1, you might decide that you will go online today and research healthy foods. Set aside a limited amount of time (perhaps 20-30 minutes) and get started. Having accomplished your goal for the day, you can be proud of yourself for your self-discipline.

TASK: Write down the step you will take today or tomorrow.

EXERCISE 3D – SELF-DISCIPLINE, ERODING

Exercise 3 provides some times to keep from getting distracted. First, write down what you intend to do and when you intend to do it. Mark that time out on your calendar so it is set aside for you to focus only on this one action. Second, remind yourself why this is important to you. If we use the example from Exercise 1, you will keep in mind that you want to eat healthier food because you have been feeling poorly and were told by your doctor that healthy food will give you energy. You like the idea of having more energy so you are motivated to eat healthier food. Third, avoid distractions. It is inevitable that things will come up that can distract you from following through on the thing you put on your calendar.

TASK: Make an agreement with yourself that whatever you commit to do you will do unless some emergency gets in the way. This is making a promise to yourself. Practice this week avoiding distractions using these tips.

EXERCISE 4D – SELF-DISCIPLINE, ERODING

Exercise 4 invites you to build on small successes. Your self-discipline will improve as you practice keeping your agreements to yourself. Every day that you create an agreement with yourself and keep it builds your integrity and your sense of pride in how you are taking care of yourself. This record of doing what you said you would do is a great asset in resisting distractions and dealing with obstacles. You won't want to undermine your growing sense of self-confidence, self-esteem, and pride.

TASK: Write down every one of your accomplishments in a diary or file. Add to it every day. You will find your growing successes a real source of strength in your life.

FACTOR – SELF-DISCIPLINE

Able to stay focused on their goals and plans even when circumstances are difficult.

SELF-ASSESSED RATING – TREADING WATER

You have sufficient discipline to maintain the life you have built for yourself.

SESSION 1

EXERCISE 1A – SELF-DISCIPLINE, TREADING WATER

You are treading water in your life primarily because, while you have sufficient self-discipline to maintain the positive aspects of your life, you can't seem to discipline yourself to move forward. You may have noticed this pattern in your life but not known how to resolve it. These exercises are designed to assist you in understanding what keeps you stuck and how you can bolster your self-discipline in order to move forward. Session 1 focuses on creating greater awareness of the gaps in your self-discipline. Let's get started.

Exercise 1 invites you to notice how well your self-discipline functions when you are at risk of losing something that is important to you. It is likely that threat mobilizes you into action. The risk of losing your job or your spouse threatening divorce gets your attention and moves you toward action. Whereas you might have been a bit lazy, suddenly you are making lists of things that need to be done and are reliably checking them off. It is good to see that you know how to discipline yourself. It is unfortunate that you need some threat in your life to jumpstart it.

TASK: List five times when threat mobilized your self-discipline.

EXERCISE 2A – SELF-DISCIPLINE, TREADING WATER

Exercise 2 invites you to notice how you seem to lack the discipline necessary to advance your life from its current state. You might notice that you have been coasting for quite some time. Your friends have been getting promotions or buying bigger houses but you haven't made many positive changes in your life at all. If you are honest with yourself, you might admit that you seem to lack ambition to do more. Without ambition it is almost impossible to harness your resources and discipline yourself to do all that will need to be done. What has happened to your ambition over the years? When did you stop wanting more? Why have you grown complacent and content?

TASK: Write down your answers.

EXERCISE 3A – SELF-DISCIPLINE, TREADING WATER

Exercise 3 invites you to see how you imagine making your life better to be difficult and full of obstacles. The future is unknown to all of us, so we all have stories about what we imagine it has in store. Your stories can be motivating. You could imagine your next job will be much more fun and will pay you enough extra money that you can travel. Or, your stories can be demotivating. You can imagine that you will keep trying to get that next job but will always lose out to someone better qualified. If your stories sap your motivation, you will have a difficult time harnessing your self-discipline.

TASK: Write down five stories you have about your future. Then notice if they are stories that motivate or demotivate you.

EXERCISE 4A – SELF-DISCIPLINE, TREADING WATER

Exercise 4 invites you to notice that too often you give up too quickly. You may have tried to advance your life quite a few times only to meet some obstacle that seemed too hard to resolve and so you gave up. There may be times when you hit problems that can't be solved, but far more often, if you persevere, you can find a way over, around, or through whatever stands in your path. Sometimes it just takes some out-of-the-box, creative thinking, but if you have given up too soon too many times, you may have undermined your belief that with enough effort and persistence you can overcome. The result is that you don't tend to try because you don't believe you have what it takes to complete what you start.

TASK: List five projects you have taken on but not completed. What stopped you? How could you have overcome the obstacle if you had persisted?

SESSION 2
EXERCISE 1B – SELF-DISCIPLINE, TREADING WATER

Session 2 focuses your attention on the basic skills of self-discipline, so you understand the key components and how they can be utilized to expand your life. Let's get started.

Exercise 1 invites you to consider the value of wanting something you don't have. Everything you have accomplished in your life is the result of having wanted something. If you are married, it is because you wanted to be in a committed relationship. If you own a home, it is because at some point home ownership had strong appeal to you. The foundation of self-discipline is desire. The greater the desire, the greater the motivation to be self-disciplined. The less the desire, the more difficult it is to stay on course.

TASK: Look back over your life and list five major accomplishments. Can you identify the desire that drove them? Next, consider your future. What do you want for your life that you don't have? How much passion do you have to reach those goals?

EXERCISE 2B – SELF-DISCIPLINE, TREADING WATER

Exercise 2 invites you to consider the importance of organization to self-discipline. The word discipline means "the practice of training people to obey rules or a code of behavior, using punishment to correct disobedience." You must have some rule, code of behavior, or plan in order to have discipline. The idea of wanting something you don't have isn't sufficient to elicit discipline. It is only when you have a plan of how you intend to achieve a goal that you have something to discipline yourself to. For example, the intention to lose 20 pounds isn't enough to discipline yourself, but when you decide you will eat only 1,500 calories per day for the next six months, you now have a sufficient tool to deploy self-discipline. You have used organization and planning in your past to discipline your choices. You may not be used to doing so with plans for your future.

TASK: Write down three things you want that you currently don't have. What are your plans to achieve those goals? If you don't have plans, create them.

EXERCISE 3B – SELF-DISCIPLINE, TREADING WATER

Exercise 3 invites you to consider the importance of the ability to delay gratification. The third aspect of self-discipline is the ability to put off what you want in the moment for the satisfaction of a goal in the future. This is a critical skill, because life is filled with interests and desires that compete for your attention. If you are distracted by whatever comes your way, you won't be able to stay on course toward your goal. You may have a plan to limit your daily calories to 1,500, but to do so you must be able to pass the donut shop without buying and eating a donut. If you can't do that, you won't succeed in losing weight.

TASK: Evaluate your ability to delay gratification from 1 (very skilled) to 5 (very poor).

EXERCISE 4B – SELF-DISCIPLINE, TREADING WATER

Exercise 4 invites you to consider the value of rewards and punishment in self-discipline. The fourth aspect of self-discipline is consequences. In order to delay gratification and stay the course, you must be able to sustain motivation and focus. Rewards and punishment are necessary tools in doing so. Rewards can be as simple as self-affirmation. When you walk past the donut shop without buying anything, you might feel good about yourself for sticking with your plan. That good feeling rewards the choice. Or, if you buy a donut and eat it, you might feel bad and regretful about your choice. That bad feeling should make it more difficult to repeat the choice you just made. You may not realize all of the subtle rewards and punishments you use throughout your day.

TASK: Make a list of five rewards and five punishments you have used this week.

SESSION 3
EXERCISE 1C – SELF-DISCIPLINE, TREADING WATER

Session 3 focuses your attention on four ways you might be undermining your self-discipline without knowing you are doing so. If you have been stuck in the same place for quite some time, it is likely that you have some issue that is hampering your natural progress. Let's see if we can't identify it. Let's get started.

Exercise 1 invites you to consider if you differentiate well between what you truly want from what you think you should want for your life. These can be very different lists. You may have numerous expectations for yourself as to how successful you should be at this stage of your life. You might feel good about what you have achieved and still have some gnawing feeling that you should be in a better situation. Rarely are goals based on what you think you should have achieved or should want adequate to elicit sufficient self-discipline to accomplish them.

TASK: To get yourself unstuck, you must be able to leave behind all expectations in order to get very clear about what truly matters to you. Sometimes those expectations can so cloud your awareness, that, until they are left behind, you won't have much motivation at all.

EXERCISE 2C – SELF-DISCIPLINE, TREADING WATER

Exercise 2 invites you to differentiate what you want for yourself versus what others want for you. You may have people who love you and care about you and who have many expectations as to who you should be and what you should do. Their voices may have motivated you to do things in the past. You may have gone to the school they recommended or started down the career path they thought was the best one for you, but in the process of listening to and pleasing them, you lost track of your voice—of what you wanted for yourself. Now you find yourself at a place where you can hardly hear your voice because it has grown so quiet. Until you find something, anything, that really matters to you, you will have no need for the self-discipline that is so critical for taking you to a new level.

TASK: Make a list of the expectations others have had for you. What do you want for yourself that isn't on that list?

EXERCISE 3C – SELF-DISCIPLINE, TREADING WATER

Exercise 3 invites you to notice the appeal of things that are easy to achieve. You may have gotten where you are because you have taken on issues that have been fairly easy to achieve. While they are valuable goals, they didn't require that much self-discipline. Now, you are facing more challenging goals; achievements that may require much more hard work and sacrifice on your part. You may be finding that the degree of self-discipline you have had isn't sufficient for these tougher challenges. As a result, you have stopped growing. You will need to either sign up for greater self-discipline or stay where you are. If that is your choice, what will you choose? Be honest with yourself. Are you willing, at this point in your life, to focus, deny yourself, and do what needs to be done to get to the next level?

TASK: If not, that is okay, but you should accept your current circumstance without complaint. If you are, get ready for change.

EXERCISE 4C – SELF-DISCIPLINE, TREADING WATER

Exercise 4 invites you to notice how you react to challenges and goals that require significant risk. Risk is a unique obstacle to change because it includes the very real possibility of losing what you have in order to gain what you want. You have done well and accomplished a lot in your life. While there might be things you still want to accomplish, you may be at a place where you aren't willing to put much at risk to make the necessary changes. If that is the case, your self-discipline won't be very useful, because you aren't willing to take on that new and risky thing. You might want to go back to school but would need to take out a loan. Are you willing to go into debt to get the degree? You may need to move to get that new job. Are you willing to leave the comfort of friends and family to pursue your dream?

TASK: Make a list of any goals you have avoided because they seemed too risky. Are you facing any now?

SESSION 4
EXERCISE 1D – SELF-DISCIPLINE, TREADING WATER

Session 4 focuses on some concrete changes you can make to strengthen your self-discipline and to focus on taking on more challenging, growth-oriented goals. Let's get started.

Exercise 1 invites you to be around people who have ambitious dreams and strong self-discipline. There is nothing like the support of a group when you need greater self-discipline. If you want to start working out, get a partner who will meet you at the gym and work out with you. If you want to learn to ski, join a ski club. You will find that you take greater risks, push yourself harder, and stick with challenges more often if you are with a group of people who are challenging themselves.

TASK: Make a list of three goals you want to take on. Write down how you can get involved with a group of people who will support you in achieving your goal.

EXERCISE 2D – SELF-DISCIPLINE, TREADING WATER

Exercise 2 invites you to write down your plans and share them with others. Goals that you don't write down leave you a lot of room to cheat. Goals you write down are clear and visible. It is obvious when you weren't self-disciplined. Don't set out to do anything without creating a plan with a checklist. Review your checklist at least once per day. It will show you exactly what you committed to do and give you the place to check the box that you did it. Remember the goal of limiting your caloric intake to 1,500 calories per day? At the end of every meal, you will write down exactly what you ate and the portion size. You will then convert your meal to calories and total them. At every meal you will know how many calories you can still consume and hit your goal. Tools like this are critical to utilizing and strengthening your self-discipline. They give you clear milestones and measuring tools.

TASK: Take one goal you have for yourself and create such a plan and checklist. Begin using it.

EXERCISE 3D – SELF-DISCIPLINE, TREADING WATER

Exercise 3 invites you to track your progress. Noting that you are moving toward your goal creates a sense of satisfaction that can become greater than the sacrifice involved in your self-discipline. Every morning that you get on the scale and see that you weigh less than you did yesterday will make it a little bit easier to bypass the donut shop without stopping in. Tracking that progress and keeping it visible is a helpful way to make it even more useful. You hang that bathing suit you plan to wear this summer on the back of your door and next to it is your weight chart. Every time you write down your new weight you can see yourself fitting into that suit. Any kind of chart that marks your progress will be encouraging and useful. You will find yourself expanding your self-discipline as a result of using it.

TASK: Create a chart for one of your important goals.

EXERCISE 4D – SELF-DISCIPLINE, TREADING WATER

Exercise 4 invites you to manage slips with kindness and grace. Self-discipline needs to have room for times when you make mistakes and revert to bad habits. It would be terribly unfortunate if you gave up on your diet because you ate one donut or if you quit school because you failed one test. Strong self-discipline is rigid enough to keep you on course but flexible enough to invite you back on the journey when you go astray. It is often wise whenever you have a lapse in discipline to ask what lesson you have to learn from the lapse that will make it less likely to happen again. Perhaps you could take a different route to work that doesn't take you by the donut shop. Or perhaps you could study for your test in the morning when you are fresh instead of after work when you are tired. Forgiveness, grace, and kindness toward yourself are extremely helpful.

TASK: Write down whatever lapses you have had. Practice forgiving yourself and inviting yourself to get back on track.

FACTOR – SELF-DISCIPLINE

Able to stay focused on their goals and plans even when circumstances are difficult.

SELF-ASSESSED RATING – GROWING

You have enough discipline to move forward and to make your life better but still maintain some areas where you are undisciplined.

SESSION 1

EXERCISE 1A – SELF-DISCIPLINE, GROWING

You are growing in your life largely because you have developed strong self-discipline that allows you to take on challenging goals and to stay on track even when things are difficult. However, you are not yet thriving because you aren't applying your self-discipline to every area of your life. Session 1 focuses on reviewing the basics of self-discipline so you can celebrate how it has been working in your life to this point. Let's get started.

Exercise 1 invites you to make the connection between having goals that are meaningful to you and your discipline to follow through. You have learned that only when you truly care about your goals and see how achieving them will enhance your life do you muster the self-discipline to follow through to the end. You will see later why this connection is relevant to your lack of thriving, but for now it is enough for you to recognize how your passion for your goals and your strong self-discipline are related.

TASK: Take a few minutes and write down three goals you have achieved in your life. Next, list three examples for each of the times you had to use self-discipline to achieve them.

EXERCISE 2A – SELF-DISCIPLINE, GROWING

Exercise 2 invites you to connect your habit of making clear plans for your goals with your strong self-discipline. It is very difficult to discipline yourself to follow a course that is unclear or absent. You have learned that the clearer you are, the more your goals are broken down into small steps, and the easier it is to discipline yourself to follow it. You may have taken on a goal such as being debt-free. Your plan included paying off your high-interest debts first and then working your way down to your low-interest debts. You decided how much you would spend to pay off your debt each week. You determined what you would cut out of your daily expenses in order to have the extra money. Because your plan was clear, each day you knew precisely what you needed to do (and not do) to make it work.

TASK: Take one goal you have achieved and write down the plan you used to achieve it.

EXERCISE 3A – SELF-DISCIPLINE, GROWING

Exercise 3 invites you to recall the tools you have used to stay focused on your goals. There are many tools people use to keep their goals front of mind. Some people carry their plan with them wherever they go. Some use checklists. Others create dream boards. Some carry a pebble in their pocket to remind them to stay focused. You have figured out which tools are most useful to you and you use them to remind yourself constantly to stay on course. This is critical because there are so many things that can distract you. You might plan to lose weight but get tempted by that donut. Or you might want to cut down on your consumption of alcohol, but you are at the game and caught up in all of the excitement. In such times, your reminder can keep your self-discipline intact.

TASK: Write down the tools you have used to stay focused. Which ones have worked best for you?

EXERCISE 4A – SELF-DISCIPLINE, GROWING

Exercise 4 invites you to notice your self-talk and how it relates to your self-discipline. Everyone talks to him or herself much of the time. Because it becomes such a part of your routine, it is easy to overlook it and to not pay attention to the messages you give yourself. Self-discipline thrives on self-talk that is positive and supportive for the most part, but also tough and demanding when needed. The right combination of carrot and stick is critical to strong self-discipline. If you are too accepting, your self-discipline may lapse when things get tough. If you are too harsh, your self-discipline may give up and quit.

TASK: Spend the next few days paying attention to your self-talk, particularly as it relates to your self-discipline. Write down the messages you send yourself. Notice if they seem to have the right balance of support and challenge.

SESSION 2
EXERCISE 1B – SELF-DISCIPLINE, GROWING

Session 2 focuses on how you have used your self-discipline to make your life better. It is so important that you see the value your self-discipline has contributed to your success, so you will be encouraged to apply it to areas you might be avoiding. Let's get started.

Exercise 1 invites you to see how your self-discipline has kept you from allowing your life to fall into disrepair. Life isn't easy for anyone. You have had your challenges—times when it took courage and perseverance to get through. You may have watched others who lacked your self-discipline falter and fail while you kept moving forward. This mental toughness has served you well. It is a resource you lean on when you face difficulties. It is also a source of confidence, because you know it is there whenever you need it.

TASK: We invite you to celebrate the toughness your self-discipline has given you by recalling some times when it would have been easy to quit but you persevered.

EXERCISE 2B – SELF-DISCIPLINE, GROWING

Exercise 2 invites you to see some of the great accomplishments you have achieved because you had the confidence in yourself to engage in challenging opportunities and to face obstacles with the belief you could overcome them. You may have friends who wouldn't have taken on some of the opportunities you have embraced because they didn't believe they could get through the challenges involved. Almost all of your accomplishments required a great deal of self-discipline. Perhaps one of your greatest accomplishments is how your children turned out. Take a few moments to remember how many things you did for them that were very difficult and demanding and how faithful you were in doing them.

TASK: Make a list of the five accomplishments of which you are most proud. Next to each, write down three instances where your self-discipline was necessary to succeed.

EXERCISE 3B – SELF-DISCIPLINE, GROWING

Exercise 3 invites you to see how your self-discipline has shaped your character. Because you have followed through on your commitments and learned how to deal with adversity without quitting or giving in, your character has been shaped and molded in ways that serve you well. You have become reliable, trustworthy, and dependable. Those character traits are ones that make you extremely useful and valuable in the world. These are traits that will win you bigger opportunities in the workplace. They are also traits that are valued socially. People like being friends with someone they can count on.

TASK: Take some time to consider what words people would use to describe your character if they could pick only five. Write them down. Can you see how at least some of these have been shaped by your self-discipline?

EXERCISE 4B – SELF-DISCIPLINE, GROWING

Exercise 4 invites you to see how the development of your self-discipline expands your future opportunities. If you are reliable with what you have now, more opportunity will be given to you. Your self-discipline earns you expansion and growth. In this way, your self-discipline opens doors for you to keep growing. It is important to see that the challenges you took on many years ago and completed paved the way for the challenges you have now. It is because you did a great job with the work you were given in your entry-level position that you were offered a promotion. Your boss saw you as someone who could be counted on to figure things out, to stick with the task, to solve problems, and to stay with things to the end, so she gave you more responsibility.

TASK: Take a few minutes and chart the opportunities you have gotten because of your self-discipline. Notice how they progressively expanded.

SESSION 3
EXERCISE 1C – SELF-DISCIPLINE, GROWING

Session 3 focuses on ways you might be holding back on the use of your self-discipline and are limiting your thriving. We will explore four possibilities. Let's get started.

Exercise 1 invites you to consider the impact of accepting some limitations in your self-discipline. You have accomplished a lot. You have been through many difficulties and pushed through to success. Perhaps you are saying to yourself something like, *Enough is enough. I am tired of saying no to myself. I am weary of putting off my gratification until later.* Yet, what you might not see is that by putting the brakes on your self-discipline, you are putting the brakes on your growth as well. Your life isn't going to change very much unless and until you change it. Changing it will always require taking on new challenges, overcoming new obstacles, learning new skills, and giving up things that have become comfortable and easy. It is your self-discipline that can push you through those changes. Are you ready to quit, to coast, to slide? If not, you need to sign up to keep growing and to continue to cultivate and develop your self-discipline.

TASK: Rate your level of desire for more from 1 (very high) to 5 (very low). Are you happy with your rating?

EXERCISE 2C – SELF-DISCIPLINE, GROWING

Exercise 2 invites you to consider any laziness you have been accepting and/or indulging. Laziness is the enemy of self-discipline. Laziness is built on the choice to take it easy over making things better. Laziness can grow gradually and without your even noticing it. It is sometimes a bigger problem for those who are relatively successful because success provides a level of comfort and ease. You can, if you choose, continue as you are without changing much of anything and life will be okay. Or, you can confront your laziness and replace it with ambitious goals that get you in action and force the cultivation of your self-discipline. Of course, the choice is yours.

TASK: Rate your level of laziness from 1 (very low) to 5 (very high). List five ways that you tend to be lazy. Consider what you might replace your laziness with that would enhance your life.

EXERCISE 3C – SELF-DISCIPLINE, GROWING

Exercise 3 invites you to consider the possibility that you are not currently using all of your self-discipline to move forward, because you are aware of the difficulties ahead of you, and your anxiety about the future is holding you back. Even though you have taken on challenges before and pressed through them, these look bigger and more difficult. You aren't certain you are up to the challenge and so you find yourself holding back rather than pushing forward. You may sense that if you get the new job you have earned a good chance of securing, your life will be turned upside down. The job includes international travel, and your life has been built around where you live. You will have to change a lot of things and you find yourself frightened as you think about it. Fear could be holding you back from pressing forward.

TASK: List any issues about the future and where you might want to go that scare you.

EXERCISE 4C – SELF-DISCIPLINE, GROWING

Exercise 4 invites you to consider the possibility that you have some sacred cows that are limiting your use of your self-discipline to change your life for the better. It is easy to acquire sacred cows: things, people, or circumstances that you are very reluctant to deal with for a variety of reasons. Even though you have been through a lot of change in your life, you won't do anything that might upset your spouse. When he gets mad, he doesn't get over it and will make your life miserable. You really want to move to a different neighborhood and know that change would open up a lot of opportunities, but you haven't brought up the idea because you don't want to upset him. Or, your parents had always wanted you to be an accountant. You have been in accounting for a long time and know it isn't for you. Even though you are excited to try something new, you don't want to hurt their feelings or run the risk of failing at something new and having them tell you they told you so. Sacred cows will hold you back. You need to use the toughness of your self-discipline to deal with each one and to eliminate their influence when it holds you back from your journey.

TASK: Make a list of all of your sacred cows.

SESSION 4

EXERCISE 1D – SELF-DISCIPLINE, GROWING

Session 4 focuses on four commitments that can help you strengthen your self-discipline and to apply it to whatever issues need to be addressed in order for you to move from growing to thriving. Let's get started.

Exercise 1 invites you to consider the commitment to being fully yourself. Self-discipline is at its essence a radical commitment to live the life you were meant to live, to live your life without compromise. It is a radical commitment because it is one not many people seem willing to make. It is so much easier to settle for comfort or mediocrity. It is always tempting to avoid conflict, problems, and difficulties by accepting things as they are. We are inviting you to something bigger—to the belief that your life is very special and that you must be the one who is so committed to living up to your full potential and to cultivating your uniqueness that you will take on whatever challenges are necessary.

TASK: Notice if you have that commitment now. It will be demonstrated in your choices. If not, are you willing to take on this commitment?

EXERCISE 2D – SELF-DISCIPLINE, GROWING

Exercise 2 invites you to commit to making your big dream clear and detailed. Will you dare to dream a big dream for your life? Will you throw off your fears and smallness and create a dream for your life based only on possibilities and without awareness of obstacles? What would you do if you could do anything? What would you do with your life if you used all of your potential? Where would you live? With whom would you connect? Dare to dream a big dream and then to create the roadmap to get there. This might be even harder than creating the dream. It is in creating the roadmap that you begin to create a sense of responsibility to make the dream happen. It is only when you have completed the roadmap that your self-discipline can engage and begin crafting the change that is needed to get from where you are to where you want to go. This is the step from growing to thriving. Everyone who is thriving has taken this step.

TASK: Decide if you are willing. If so, write down your dream and create your plan.

EXERCISE 3D – SELF-DISCIPLINE, GROWING

Exercise 3 invites you to commit to surrounding yourself with the very best. If you are going to be your very best, you need to surround yourself with people who think and behave like you. The people in your life shape your life. They are either anchors that hold you back or oars that propel you forward. If you are going to live up to your potential, you will need to be selective as to whom you add to your network, and you will always need to be willing to leave behind those who can't keep up. This can be difficult, but it is very important.

TASK: Write down the names of the people who are currently in your network. Next to each name indicate if they are an anchor (A) or an oar (O). Next, make a list of people who should be added to your network because they can make a valuable contribution to your journey. Invite them. Finally, consider how you will eliminate those who are anchors and get it done.

EXERCISE 4D – SELF-DISCIPLINE, GROWING

Exercise 4 invites you to commit to burn your boats. Sometimes in life you need to cut off your path of retreat so the only option is to move forward. When you do this, you commit to your self-discipline. You can't back up. You can only move forward. Now your self-discipline shifts from being optional to being necessary. Sometimes burning your boats might seem irrational or foolish. You might buy the house you want even before you sold the one you have because you know it needs to be done. You might quit your job before you have the next one because you need to be in a different city to audition. Burning the boats is a powerful thing. Perhaps you have done so at other times in your life.

TASK: If so, list them. How did things turn out? Chances are they turned out well.

Made in the USA
Columbia, SC
14 January 2018